MW00617508

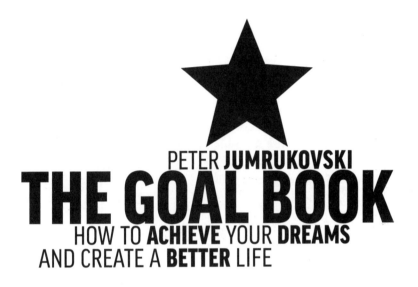

PETER **JUMRUKOVSKI**

THE GOAL BOOK

HOW TO **ACHIEVE** YOUR **DREAMS**
AND CREATE A **BETTER** LIFE

#thegoalbook

THE GOAL BOOK: How to Achieve Your Dreams and Create a
Better Life.
© 2016 by Peter Jumrukovski
All rights reserved.

This publication is designed to provide competent and reliable information regarding the subject matters covered. However, it is sold with the understanding that the author and publisher are not engaged in rendering legal, financial or other professional advice. Laws and practices often vary from state to state and country to country and if legal or other expert assistance is required, the services of a professional should be sought. The author and publisher specifically disclaim any liability that is incurred from the use or application of the contents of this book.

The Goal Book is available at special discounts for bulk purchases by corporations, institutions, and other organizations. For more information, please visit www.thegoalbook.com or e-mail info@ilsuccess.com.

I Love Success
www.thegoalbook.com

Editor: Erika Feldt
Translation: Josephine Burdon
Portrait: Anders Roos
Printed in the United States of America
ISBN: 978-0-692-61598-0

Contact:
info@ilsuccess.com

I Love Success
312 Arizona Ave.
Santa Monica, CA 90401

THANKS

... to the best family in the world.

Thank you **mom Violeta** for always being there and for always giving everything to the family.
Thank you **to my father Slafko**, for all the support throughout the years.
Thank you **my sister Julijana**, your book inspired me to write this book.
Thank you **Lilian** for coming into my life and for having been there all the way.

Thanks to **my closest friends**, you know who you are. You make life fun to live.

Thank you **karate** for showing me the world.

Thank you **Sweden**, for all the great opportunities.

Thank you **USA**, for believing in me and giving me a chance to create the life of my dreams.

Last but not least: thanks to all of you who believed in me and a special thanks to all the haters, you make me fight even harder.

/Peter Jumrukovski

CONTENTS

PREFACE

Today is a really nice Swedish spring day; the sun is shining, the birds are singing and the air has that wonderful scent. It's somewhat colder than usual and the winter has been extra tough this year, at least to me. Today, I find myself in the most beautiful library we have in our country. I'm sitting alone at a gray round table with four green chairs. The view I have in front of me is the Nissan, a truly beautiful river that flows into the Kattegat. The water flows slowly and continuously. The thought strikes me that life is like water – slowly but surely it goes its steady course. If you have a plan you can control life in the direction you want, if not you risk that life takes on a different direction. It has happened to me a couple of times that life has taken a turn that I have not expected. How can that be, I wonder?

The answer is in this book. Within each of us there is great potential to achieve the goals we have and realize our dreams. The ability is there but many of us do not really know where to start. How do you actually go about to live a life of happiness, well-being and wealth?

I would be lying if I said that it would be enough to only read this book, it is absolutely not. However, if you are willing to do what I suggest, there are no limits to what you can achieve in your life.

For a long time I have searched in the jungle of self-help books for a book in which there is a simple guide to what I should do to achieve success in different parts of life: health, money, personality, relationships and socially. When I didn't find such a book, I decided to write one myself. Here you will learn how to bring out the best in you and create a rewarding and successful life in all its parts.

Good luck with your goals, I know that you can succeed!

/Peter Jumrukovski

INTRODUCTION

Congratulations, you have just made your best investment in a long time. An investment in your own life. The Goal Book will teach you how to set goals in various parts of life and how to turn a plan into reality. Because you deserve to be healthy and feel good, you deserve financial success, you deserve to achieve what you want in your life and you deserve to have good relationships with people around you. Yes, you simply deserve to live the life that you have always dreamed about.

I believe in you and therefore I assume that you are willing to spend the time it takes to really succeed in achieving your goals. It will require a lot, but don't let that scare you. What is a little bit of work in comparison to being able to live a life in good health, with as much money as you desire and the relationships that you want, while at the same time having a strong meaning with your life?

I believe in you, there is a purpose that you picked up this book from the shelf. Now is the time for you to believe in yourself and dare to trust me by following the advice that I give in this book.

I have tried to make everything as simple and practical as possible to easily let you work your way towards your goals. Remember that this is not a book that you can simply lie in bed and read, you must be active and do the exercises and act to create the life you desire.

Now, straighten up and get ready for a new, happier and richer life.

Let's go!

WHAT IS A GOAL?

"A goal is a dream with a deadline."

/ Napoleon Hill

Every person on this planet is unique and we all have our strengths and weaknesses. But what applies to most of us is that we want to achieve something, either for ourselves, our family and friends or for other people. For a little boy from poor conditions it may be to save up to a pair of nice basketball shoes, for someone else it may be moving to Japan and becoming a businessman. Yes, the dreams and goals are many and most people have one or a few.

With my background as an elite athlete and a career as a businessman and salesperson, I have met many people with different dreams and goals. In competitive sports that is something that most people have, why compete otherwise? Obviously you compete because it's fun, but to perform on top and get that extra edge, you need to have dreams and goals. By setting different goals for yourself, it becomes easier to get through the days when your whole body aches, feel unwell and you most of all want to bury yourself underneath the covers for the rest of the day. If you have a goal, it becomes much easier to fight because you know where you are going.

But what is a goal? As Napoleon Hill, author of *Think and Grow Rich* said: "A goal is a dream with a deadline."

What did he mean by that? Well, many people have lots of dreams and goals, but they don't really know when they will become a reality and they don't do anything particular to achieve the goals.

TO MAKE THIS A LITTLE CLEARER, HERE IS AN EXAMPLE

Linda and her husband Andy have two children and live a good life in a suburb of Chicago. They are financially stable, living in a house and drive two cars. They usually go on vacation during the summer and can afford to treat themselves and their children to a lot of fun. Even though they are living a good life, Linda and Andy feel that something is missing in their lives. When they met, they had big plans. The dream was to open a small family friendly hotel in Florida. However, much like so many other people everyday life interrupted those plans and now it might never happen? The children attend school and have their friends, Linda and Andy have good jobs that keep them busy and pay their bills – even if it's not the jobs of their dreams. Linda has long had trouble sleeping at night, she wonders to herself if this is the way life should be.

Their problem is not unique. They had a dream, but what have they actually done to achieve it? The days have turned into weeks, weeks into months and months into years.

Now they feel that they are stuck. To resign from their jobs, to sell the house and move feels too difficult: "We cannot do that?"

But that is where they are wrong. A perfect time to do something in life will never come, the important thing is to learn to set a goal and then make a plan to get there. In this way, everyone can, with tiny steps, succeed.

If Linda and Andy want to succeed, they need to write down their goals and set up an action plan (activity plan) that they can follow. Only then can they realize their dream which now has become a goal.

For many people a dream is something unattainable, something you fantasize about. To turn a dream into a goal, you need to write it down and possibly split it up into sub-goals and set a deadline. When you have written down what you want to achieve and when you should achieve it, then you can start planning how to reach that goal.

Therefore, I would like to add a word to Napoleon Hill's definition of what a goal is: **"A goal is a written down dream with a deadline."**

When Linda and Andy have written down their goal and set a deadline they have to start planning to achieve the goal. They need to find out how running a hotel works, learn about rules and regulations in Florida, look up schools and opportunities for their children, create a budget, and so on.

When the plan is complete, the dream will suddenly feel more real. It will not be easy to get out of the rat race they have fallen into, but with proper planning and discipline, they will succeed.

In this book you will learn how to transform your dreams into goals. And if you don't have any dreams, you will learn how to find things that you are passionate about and what you can do to turn them into tangible goals. You will learn how to easily distinguish yourself from the masses who live a life they are not happy with, but feel powerless to change. Your days being powerless are over, you set your own limits, and here you will receive practical tools that will help you achieve your goals.

HOW JAYDEN GOT HIS DREAM BIKE

Jayden is an American nine-year-old boy who loves to draw and play Playstation. He is raised in an ordinary American family in California. One day, Jayden comes home from school and says, "Daddy, Daddy! Noah got a bike and I want one too, it's super stylish, has 18 gears and you can do tricks with it." Jayden's father is a businessman and has learned to fight for what you want in life, therefore he also wants to teach his son how you can use your own knowledge to get what you want in life. He decides that it's time to teach Jayden how he can get his dream bike and other things he wants in life, simply by setting goals and working towards them.

"Okay, Jayden, what does the bike cost?" asks the father. Jayden says that the bike costs $140 and that's really cheap. It's the neatest and best bike that Jayden has ever seen. The dad sees the glow in Jayden's eyes and for a brief second, he wants to go to the bike shop and buy the bike right away, but he restrains himself.

Dad tells Jayden that he will not buy the bike but he will help him find a way to save up for it. They should set a goal and work towards it. Jayden gets upset – his best friend got the bike right away – but because he has no choice he has to play along.

THIS IS WHAT JAYDEN'S GOAL LOOKS LIKE

Date: March 1, 2015
Goal: Save $140 before June 1, 2015 in order to be able to buy my dream bike.

Now that Jayden has set his goal, he thinks it seems impossible. He has never seen so much money.

Then Jayden's dad says that it will be easier to achieve the goal if it's divided into sub-goals.

"Between March 1 and June 1 it's 14 weeks," says Jayden's dad. "How much do you need to save per week Jayden?"

Jayden who is good at math quickly calculates that $140/14 weeks = $10 per week.

Sub-goal: Save $10 per week. Since Jayden knows he gets $10 as a weekly allowance, he immediately gets happy.

"Daddy, Daddy! If I save all my weekly allowance I can afford to buy the bike!"

This was the story of how Jayden achieved his goal of get-

ᶜᵉ ☆ ᶜᵉ

NO MATTER WHAT YOU WANT TO ACHIEVE OR DEVELOP

in your life, you need to plan how you will get there. By sitting down and making a plan you can increase your chances significantly.

ting his dream bike. The example may seem very simple, but that is the way it works. It's time to stop talking about dreams and instead begin to turn them into goals and sub-goals with action plans. As long as you know what you want and how to get there you can get exactly what you wish for.

DO YOUR HOMEWORK

"He who fails to plan is planning to fail."
/ Winston Churchill

Now you might be thinking that if it's so easy to accomplish your goals, how can it be that so many people never achieve what they want? There are several answers to this question, but the two biggest reasons are:

*   You have the wrong goal or action plan.
*   You don't do your homework.

Many people out there who don't succeed reaching their goals have probably made it too difficult for themselves, they have set an unrealistic goal or created an unworkable action plan. It's important that the goals are motivating (more on this later), in other words, you should know that by achieving your goal something is added to your life. It's also important that your plan is possible to carry through and that you are able to do what is required of you to succeed.

EXAMPLE

Goal: Lose 20 lbs in ten weeks.
Sub-goal: To lose two lbs per week.
Action plan: Work out two sessions per day, eat a healthy diet and sleep at least six hours per night.

This action plan might work for a super motivated person with a lot of spare time. If you have children, a partner and two jobs this action plan is probably too optimistic and what happens then? Well, it gets too tough and you give up. When this kind of situation occurs – and it will occur – it's important that you don't give up. Instead, it's time to change the plan to something that works for you. It's important to be flexible and find a way that suits you and your life situation.

Therefore it's important that you think through your goals and make sure they are motivating, tough and achievable. By continuing to read and work with this book you will learn how to set goals that lifts you up and gives you a happier and more successful life.

The other big reason why you don't succeed with your goals is that you don't do your homework. Now you are probably wondering what I mean by that? Not doing your homework can mean different things. What most people find difficult when it comes to working towards a goal is to get their new routines to fit into their everyday life. You might recognize this? New Year's resolution to quit smoking, lose weight or find a new job doesn't last for more than a few weeks, then you fall back into your old routines. That is one of many examples of not doing your homework. It's so easy to fall into old and bad habits if you are not sufficiently disciplined.

Many of us quit when it gets tough, when we have a headache, when we are too stressed or just don't feel like it. Unfortunately, the reality is that you have to fight for good things and if you want to achieve your goals you must take small steps every day. If you are not willing to change, it will be difficult for you to move on in life and work with yourself and your goals.

The great thing is that if you learn how to work with goals each day there are no limits to what you can accomplish. Small, small steps each day add up and turns into fantastic results in the end..

Think about what small daily actions can do for you to succeed with something. A brick may not look like much to the world when you hold it in your hand, but a house is the result of many small actions. Brick by brick, the house has been built.

That's why it's absolutely vital that you learn to set a plan and follow it every single day. Don't cheat, then you are only fooling yourself and it will be hard to get back on track.

Imagine that you are a builder and want to build a house. You have figured out that the house will consist of 1 000 bricks and that you should be done in 100 days. Your goal is to lay ten bricks a day (1 000 bricks/100 days = ten bricks/day).

EXAMPLE

Goal: Build a house consisting of 1 000 bricks in 100 days.
Sub-goal: Lay ten bricks a day.
Result: A beautiful house that I can sell and make money on.

Your goal is consequently to add ten bricks per day, if you do that you have finished building the house in 100 days.

What happens if you are not doing your daily job for a week? Well, then you have missed to lay 70 bricks (seven days x ten bricks = 70 bricks).

And what happens if you only lay eight bricks a day? All of a sudden it will take you 125 days to build the house (1000 bricks/8 = 125 days).

As you can see, the end result is highly dependent on your job performance. If you put yourself in the situation and play with the idea that you have the house in front of you, you realize quickly that every brick counts. The same goes with your goals in life, if you skip your homework one day, you reduce your chances to succeed. The mistake many people make is that they ignore their homework for way too long and suddenly that goal feels distant and demotivating.

Sometimes, however everyday life takes over and something happens that makes it impossible to follow through with your goals and do the homework. If that happens to you, try as quickly as possible to go back to doing your homework, the longer time it takes for you to get back to working towards your goal, the harder it will be for you to succeed. If you completely fall out of sync and fail doing your homework for far too long, sit down and reformulate your goals to fit your everyday life. It's also important that you understand that if you do the same thing you did yesterday, you will get the same results that you got yesterday.

The famous words by one of the absolute greatest football players of all time Jerry Rice: "Today I will do what others won't, so tomorrow I can accomplish what others can't" are appropriate words in this context. Make sure to establish necessary discipline to be able to do your homework every day. And remember that just as a house is built brick by brick, you will reach your goals one step at a time.

WHY YOU SHOULD WRITE DOWN YOUR GOALS

1979 a study was done about goals at the prestigious Harvard University in the United States. It's one of the toughest schools to get into and those who are accepted are all hard working and intelligent students who are expected to have fantastic careers ahead of them. Average starting salary for a Harvard student who enters the work force is about $115,000 per year.

It was the 1979 graduating class at Harvard University who got interviewed. It was found that:

* 84 percent had no specific goals.
* 13 percent had goals, but they were not written down.
* 3 percent had clear, written down goals and plans on how to achieve them.

To measure the success of these academics they were interviewed again ten years later. The result showed that:

+ the 13 percent who had goals that were not written down earned an average of twice as much as those who had no goals at all.

+ the 3 percent who had clear written goals earned an average of ten times as much as the other 97 percent in the survey.

Essentially all of the survey participants got well-paid jobs after graduation, but the wage gap was apparently very large.

After reading this, I hope that you realize how valuable it is for you to write down your goals and develop a plan for how you will achieve them. Remember that just by reading this puts you ahead of most people out there. Even if you are not competing against others, you can with the knowledge of setting goals create the life you desire. For you, maybe it's not all about making the most money or changing your weight. Maybe you want to feel valuable in your everyday life or meet someone to share your life with, or move abroad. No matter what you want your first step is to write down what you want and how to get there. By not taking a stand on what you wish for, things can turn out any way for you – some of us are lucky in life, others are unlucky. Instead of leaving it to chance you can by setting goals build your own future and create your own luck. The possibilities are endless for those who dare to think about and write down their goals and create a plan to achieve them.

DRAW YOUR OWN LIFE MAP

Many probably dream about traveling around the world. Imagine that you have decided to make such a trip. What's the next step? You are probably thinking about which places to visit, if you intend to get there by plane, boat, train, car or any other means of transportation. You may decide how long to stay in each place and make room for changes if you like a

CHAPTER 1 🌳

particular place a lot. The next step may be to come up with a budget, in other words, see how much you can afford to spend on the trip as a whole and on each day. In the end you have planned your dream trip, you have decided which places to visit and approximately how the journey will look like and when you are leaving. So did the merchants once when they set out on their great voyages. What do you think would have happened if they didn't have a plan for the trip or didn't know where they were going? Even if they were hit by major storms, pirates, or simply sailed the wrong way (GPS didn't exist at that time) they had a plan that they followed. If anything went wrong, they had to adjust accordingly to get back to their planned route.

Just as the ancient merchants and students at Harvard, you also need to create a plan for your life's journey. No matter what you want to achieve or develop in your life you need to plan how you will get there. By sitting down and creating a plan your chances significantly increases.

In my profession as a salesman and in my career as an elite athlete, I have met thousands of people who struggle every day to achieve something great, it can be succeeding with their business or becoming a world champion in their sport. At our first meeting it's already possible to know what level of success the person in question will achieve with their current way of thinking. What distinguishes those who have been most successful is that they constantly have plans and ideas that they work with. If a plan doesn't work, they immediately make another one where they adjust what didn't go well last time. In the end they find a recipe for success that they build on.

The same applies to you. By reading this book, you will certainly avoid many of the mistakes that I and many others have made on the road to success, but you will still make your own mistakes. When you do something wrong, you can choose to

∽☆∽

REMEMBER...
*as long as you have
not given up
you have not failed.*

see it as a failure and give up, or as a lesson and adjust what is needed to do better in the future. Remember: as long as you have not given up, you have not failed. If you instead of becoming disheartened go through what you did wrong and correct it, you will become stronger in the future.

There is a story about a man whose mistakes later saved the lives of many people. There was a man named Mark who was a lifeguard on the island of Maui in Hawaii. The beach where he worked is one of the world's most beautiful beaches that during the season attracts thousands of happy people who want to sunbathe, swim and have a good time. But the beach is treacherous, the strong waves can strike when you least expect it and drag the tourists far out into the water.

Mark was a young, tough kid who loved to swim and surf and one day he and some friends decided to go to this particular beach and surf. When they got there the waves were strong and the lifeguard had forbidden all visitors to enter the water. Young and stupid (he thought he was tough) Mark decided to defy the ban and took his surfboard and threw himself into the water. Mark was a skilled surfer, he was raised in Hawaii and had surfed almost every day since he was a little boy. Despite his experience he got a bit worried when he felt the big waves and how strong the currents were. The idea of getting back to the beach hit him several times, but his friends were watching him and now he could not back down. However, it was impossible to stay on the board and time after time Mark fell into the water.. He paddled frantically in the big waves and had to give everything he could to get somewhere. Now he heard the lifeguard whistle and his friends shouted that he should come back.

Mark took charge and paddled and paddled until he saw a big wave coming from the horizon. He knew it would be his toughest match against the sea ever. The wave came closer and it was so strong that Mark did not even manage to get up on the surfboard. The wave swept over Mark who disappeared into the water. His thoughts as he was under the water were many, "Would his life end this way? Would his own foolishness kill him? He should have listened to the lifeguard's advice."

To make a long story short: Mark got washed up on the beach after three minutes. He was unconscious, but the lifeguard was able to rescue him. This event changed Mark's life and that's when he decided to become a lifeguard himself on that same beach and rescue others who are deceived by the treacherous waves. Mark saw his mistake as a lesson and decided not to allow others to make the same mistakes as him.

The story of Mark may be too extreme for your everyday life, but it shows how your mistakes can impact you to do good both for yourself and for others. The errors you make today, can shape you into a better person tomorrow. Although Mark should have been smart enough not to surf that day it led to something good in the end. I don't recommend you to be as stupid as Mark, who actually risked his life, but instead I encourage you to strive for your goals, to dare to make mistakes and move beyond what is comfortable and easy. Dare to try, dare to make mistakes and learn from them in order to bring you closer to your goals. It's easier to succeed than you think.

Most people are so afraid to fail that they dare not even try, thus competition is less among those who actually dare to do it. Dare to draw your own life map, even if you are skeptical, I'm convinced that you will succeed.

TASK 1

If you are lying comfortably on the couch or in the bed, it's now time to straighten up and take a few deep breaths. Before closing the book it's time for your first task. Whether you feel like it or not it's now you are going to do it, not in a couple of hours, tomorrow or this weekend, but NOW! To succeed with your goals, it's important that you begin your training immediately. You need about 20 minutes.

Your first task will be to set a goal that spans over ten days with a task (sub-goal) each day. Start simple – don't worry, we will advance towards your big fun goals eventually – now it's about getting into the rhythm of setting goals and have fun with it.

» Set a goal that spans ten days.
» At least one task (sub-goal) should be done daily.
» Decide on a reward to give yourself when you have succeeded.

Make sure to make the goal simple and fun. The most important thing during the next ten days is that you do something every day and learn how to get into a new routine.

EXAMPLE 1

Goal: Get stronger. Do 100 push-ups and 200 sit-ups in ten days.
Sub-goal: Do ten push-ups per day (100 push-ups/10 days = 10 push-ups/day) and 20 sit-ups per day (200 sit-ups/10 days = 20 sit-ups/day).
Reward: Eat my favorite cheesecake.

EXAMPLE 2

Goal: Do something uncomfortable: talk to ten strangers in ten days.
Sub-goal: Talk to one stranger per day.
Reward: The feeling of daring.

EXAMPLE 3

Goal: Take the family out for dinner: $150
Sub-goal: Save $15 per day ($150/10 days = $15/day).
Reward: Dinner with the family.

That was a couple of examples. Now write down your goals and go ahead and work towards them. You will feel how fun it actually is to set and work towards goals. Good luck!

Ps. Don't forget to do the exercise NOW!

ℓℓ ☆ ℓℓ

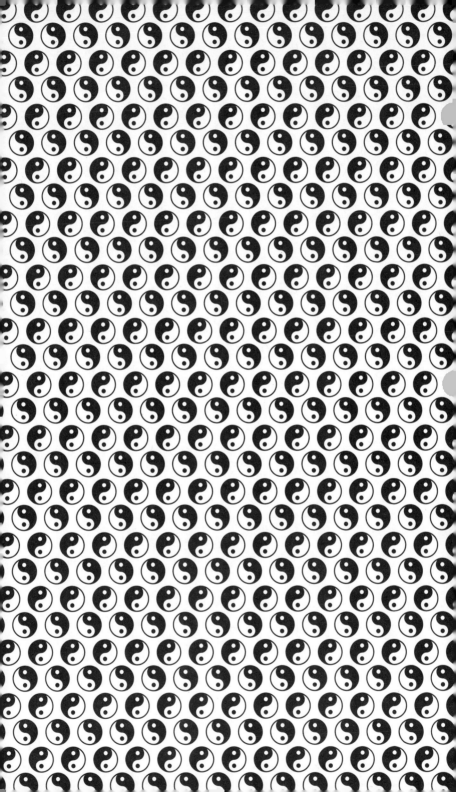

BALANCE

"Success is liking yourself, liking what you do and liking how you do it."

/ Maya Angelou

What is success? What is happiness? Is success and happiness the same thing or two different things? Have you met any successful person who doesn't seem happy? Or have you met any happy person who in the common man's eyes is not successful?

There are countless of stories of poor farmers, fishermen, housekeepers and people from poor backgrounds who talk about how happy they are, how nice families they have and how good their lives have been in spite of all the tough times. On the other hand, there are stories about wealthy and successful people living alone in their million dollar mansions. They have all the material items you could wish for but no one to share it with. You can twist and turn this as much as you want but the fact is that there are happy and unhappy people in all walks of life. Just as there are successful and less successful people everywhere.

Success and happiness is a feeling within us. Only by working with ourselves and our goals we can feel happy and successful. For example, if you set goals that are impossible for you to achieve your chances to feel successful decreases, if on the other hand you always set goals that are so easy that they don't motivate you, you will not feel successful either.

There are many people in the world that are remarkably

successful in one area, such as career, but in other areas, such as friendship and relationships, are very incomplete. To be successful in every aspect of life is one of the most difficult things, but it's also the most important thing in order to be able to live a happy life. My goal with this book is to give you the tools needed to create a happy and successful life. You will learn how you can prioritize in your life and create success, happiness and balance in the different areas of life.

WHY OLYMPIC BRONZE MEDALISTS ARE HAPPIER THAN SILVER MEDALISTS

In sports, it's clear who the winners and losers are. There is one first place (gold medalist), a second place (silver medalist) and a third place (bronze medalist), the remaining participants end up outside the podium. Logically, you should be able to say that the gold medalist is the happiest, the silver medalist second happiest and thereafter comes the bronze medalist.

There has been several studies on this subject, where Olympic athletes have been studied. The research shows that the bronze medalist generally is happier than the silver medalist. How can it be that the bronze medalist is happier than the silver medalist? Should it not be the opposite? But just as in other areas of life, it turns out that happiness depends on what you compare yourself with and what could have been. The silver medalist lost the final and although he or she is second best they compare themselves with the gold medalist. The bronze medalist, on the other hand, compare themselves with the one who came in fourth place. The bronze medalist consequently feels like a winner while the silver medalist feels like a loser.

This is a good example of how it can be in life in general. Many people are very successful, but compare themselves constantly with those who have it even better and are even more successful. It means that they are not as happy as people who instead compare themselves with someone who has it a little worse or are a little less fortunate.

In my eyes, those who are the happiest are those who compare themselves with themselves and compete against themselves: "Where was I a year ago? How have I developed in this area in the last month?"

By competing against yourself and against your own goals instead of against others, you will be much happier. It can be difficult to compare yourself to other people in a fair way since we all have different backgrounds, stories and preconditions. For you it may seem only natural to be able to walk across the street, but for someone who has been involved in a car accident and injured his leg, it can be a fantastic achievement. Your goals cannot be compared. If you compare yourself with that person your goals would become far too easy and similarly would the goals be too difficult for the injured person if he or she is comparing themselves with you.

Dare to stand on your own two feet and work towards your own goals. Compete against yourself and be sure to reward yourself and be happy with what you have achieved. By finding the joy in your goals and work towards them, you will feel a tremendous motivation and happiness during the journey. If you constantly compare yourself to other people you enter a race that you just cannot win, it's impossible to be the best at everything all the time. And does it really matter? What is important is that you feel that you are on the right track and that you are harmonious in your everyday life.

FIND YOUR BALANCE

"To be successful means to have a balance of achievements in the various areas of your life. You cannot honestly call yourself successful in your business life if your family life is in shambles."

/ Zig Ziglar

What does balance really mean? In modern society, people are talking so much about living a balanced life, even though demands on us are constantly increasing. How can you live in balance when there are so many demands on us humans? First and foremost it's important to understand that if we really want to live a happy, successful and balanced life, we must work for it. We must learn to think outside the box and rely on our own instincts. We have to dare to create the life we know deep down that we deserve. Be proud of yourself because you have decided to deal with this. When you are really old and you are approaching the end of life, don't you want to look back on your life with joy? Don't you want to think that you have lived a good life with many successes? A lot of tough moments will certainly also occur in your life, but by preparing yourself and creating a map of your life you will be much better equipped to live the life you desire.

Before you can find your balance, you need to find out which areas in your life that need to be balanced. It's different from person to person, but I will mention the things that most of us need to feel a purpose in our lives.

The areas that we need to work on to create a balance in our lives are:

* **Health.** If you don't feel well, physically or mentally, it doesn't matter how it looks like in other areas of your life. By creating good health, you have come a long way towards a balanced and successful life.

ℓℓ ☆ ℓℓ

TO BE SUCCESSFUL MEANS

*to have a balance
of achievements
in the many areas
of your life.*

* **Money.** Money is something all people need. Rent, mortgage, clothes, travel, cars, health, education, food and so on. By creating financial stability you make your life so much easier.

* **Personal Goals.** Personal goals can involve everything from your career to interests, such as sports, dream trips or a desire to play a musical instrument. By supporting your personal interests you give yourself a chance to become a happier person.

* **Relationship Goals.** Most of us want to share our success and happiness with someone. We also want someone who can support us in difficult times. Relationships also include friendship, family, colleagues and so on.

* **Social Goals.** The social goals involves how you can and want to behave towards others, how you communicate with your surroundings. There are so many nice people in the world who wish you well and by communicating in the right way, you can attract the people you want in your life.

To create a balanced life you need to work with all of the things above. By challenging yourself to develop in all these areas, you will learn a lot about yourself and create a meaningful life that includes every aspect of life. For me, success is not to just seek success in one area and "forget" about the others. I don't know if you have thought about this before, but give yourself the chance to work with all areas. If you really decide to do this, I can promise you that your life will be better in every way. Dare to spend the time it takes to get good at this thing called life, it will pay off. Imagine that you have mastered all areas, imagine that you are healthy, well and strong, imagine that you have the financial stability you desire, imagine that you are striving for your personal goals, imagine that you have good relationships in your life and the social ability to attract the people you want in your life. What more can you ask for?

Take on this challenge and you will see that the future will bring much joy. Balance is difficult. Some days you wake up on the right side, energetic and happy and everything is going your way. Those days it's easy to be balanced. But what do we do those days when we more than anything want to bury our head under the pillow and lie under the covers all day? How can I find balance those days when everything goes wrong, when I accidentally scratch a neighbor's car, get a speeding ticket or my son has had a fight in school? Interestingly, it's these days when it's most important to have confidence in yourself and have the patience to remain calm. Today is such a day for me: I have slept poorly, I'm irritated and sitting on a train instead of lying in bed, something I could pay a fortune to do right now. But despite that, I have decided to turn my imbalance into balance. We will see how it goes, but as I'm writing about this I already see how ridiculous I really am. Days like this I should think about how good I have it, what a wonderful life I live, what lovely things I get to experience and what nice people I have around me. We all have a lot of things we can be grateful for. Just as in the study of the Olympic medalists, on a day like this one can choose to see what you actually have in your life instead of focusing on what you don't have. Remember the things or memories that are worth noting and be happy about. Be grateful for the relationships you have in your life. And guess what: the things you lack in your life you can create by following the advice in this book.

Believe it or not, being in imbalance can actually help you to find balance. A few weeks ago, by mere chance, I attended a lecture. The speaker was a very interesting and funny guy. Besides that, he was also very skilled in his field as a coach for businessmen/women and sportsmen/women. He had worked with coaching for over 20 years and with his unorthodox methods he had helped many to success. To get the athletes to improve in their respective sports, he trained imbalance with them, the more imbalance they had while training, the better the balance they had in the element of competition. It's an interesting theory that works for many. By challenging ourselves and dare to fall out of balance, we can learn to deal with the really important moments in our life. So don't be afraid to fall out of balance, instead see it as a training. A training for the times when it's really important for you to be in balance.

YOU ARE THE CAPTAIN OF YOUR OWN SHIP

Imagine a ship, a big, beautiful and magnificent sailing ship. The ship symbolizes your life. You can see the ship sailing on the high seas. The sea represents the challenges and opportunities you will face. On the ship there is a big crew to ensure that it reaches its destination. The crew symbolizes the people who are around you. There is another person who is out on this voyage, it's you. It's you who is the captain of the ship. Give yourself a few minutes and think about what is required for the trip to be successful.

* The ship must have a destination. There may be several sub-destinations and the route can be changed along the way, but in order for the ship to not just drift around on the seas and eventually sink it needs to have a main destination.
* The captain of the ship must be able to steer the ship to its destination and get the crew to work with, not against him/her.

You probably know where I'm going with this story. Just as the captain of the sailing ship, you have to know where you want to steer your life and have a plan for how you will get there. It's not certain that you can know this right away, and I'm not saying it's easy. But if you don't know where you are going there is a great risk that you wake up one day and wonder where you are and where life went. Remember that all the thoughts, feelings and problems that you have, there are several other people who have had. They have had your problems, they have solved them and written books about it. So help is available for those looking for it.

The ship symbolizes your life and what is important to you. Thus you need to be the captain of your own life and make sure that the crew, the people around you, help you towards a better life and can support you when things get tough. Some days out on the open seas the sun shines and the sea is calm, other days the weather turns into a storm. It's the same in life. As the captain of your own ship, you are responsible for having the right crew that adds joy to your life, and who are good at dealing with a storm when it happens – because it will happen, sooner or later. Don't waste energy on negative people and don't try to make everyone else happy, instead make sure to do what it takes to create the life you want and the journey you want to take.

It's a great responsibility you have received, to sail this ship ashore. But quite honestly, would you want someone else to choose how your life should look like?

Perhaps you are used to making decisions, perhaps you are not. It doesn't matter how your life has been like until today, by taking in the knowledge in this book and start taking charge of your life you can create the joy, success and happiness you desire. To succeed, it's important that you dare to take responsibility and become the captain of your own life. A true captain who dares to go forward when life gets stormy but also has the awareness to enjoy life when it's good.

THE ART OF DARING TO FAIL

"Our greatest glory consists not in never falling, but in rising every time we fall."
/ Jigoro Kano

There are thousands of inspiring stories of people who continued moving forward even when everything didn't go as they wished. They have dared to stand up again and try again and again and again, as many times it has been necessary.

One of the most famous is the inventor and businessman Thomas Alva Edison. Most people know Edison as the inventor of the light bulb. What many people don't know is that he worked on it for two years day and night and made several thousand mistakes before he finally succeeded.

"I have not failed. I've just found 10,000 ways that won't work", replied Edison when asked how many times he had failed to invent the light bulb. Children have the same attitude that Thomas Edison had. Just think about how it looks when a child is learning to walk. By trying and making mistakes, the child learns what isn't working and continues forward until he/she finally can walk. Many of us have created an environment in the adult world where we cannot fail or make mistakes. If we do, we feel embarrassed and quit. This is completely crazy and if you want to create a good life, you must learn that there is nothing wrong in failing. That is simply how you learn.

THIS IS HOW YOU LEARN SOMETHING NEW
* You try.
* You make mistakes.
* You learn from it and the next time you do it a little better.

The math is simple in life: it's hard to be good at something that is completely new to you. Some have the advantage of being so called talented or easily taught, for the rest of us, it's more difficult and we'll have to try some more. The advantage in today's society is that there is so much information about everything. It means that you don't have to repeat all the mistakes yourself, but can learn by seeing how other people have done. What's important to be able to move forward and work towards your goals is to dare to make mistakes. If you look closely at many successful people and read about their path to success, you will notice that one of the biggest reasons that many of them have succeeded is that they have tried and failed many, many times before they finally succeeded.

One thing that many find difficult is what others think of us. Do you care what others think about you? Most people try in one way or another to appear talented in the eyes of others and are afraid to show their weaker sides. It's something you need to work on. Remember, at Harvard University, there were only three percent who had clear, written goals. Let us say that this number is similar in society as a whole, which means that only three of 100 people have written down their goals in life. This means that you will be unique and should not be afraid of the opinions of people who don't know what it means to work with goals. The big advantage of all this is that you will have a tremendous amount of fun on the way, you will develop and learn lots of new things. And last but not least, you will achieve your goals.

You will now receive two different tasks. The first one will train you in finding your balance and the other will train you in daring to fail. Do both and start now. Decide to spend 15 minutes to get started with these tasks, even if it feels uncomfortable. You will be richly rewarded.

TASK 1: BALANCE

    a. Rank these five areas of life. Write one in front of what's most important to you, two in front of the second most important, and so on.

ꬲ ☆ ꬲ

DON'T WASTE
ENERGY ON
NEGATIVE PEOPLE

and don't try to make
everyone else happy,
instead make sure to do
what it takes to create
the life you want
and the journey that
you want to take.

* Health
* Money
* Yourself (Personal Goals)
* Relationships
* Social life

b. Once you have ranked these areas, write down what percentage of your time you currently spend on each area.

c. Write down what percentage of your time you wish to devote to each of these areas in order to live a happy, successful and balanced life.

TASK 2: DARE TO FAIL

This exercise aims to teach you the courage to try new things without focusing on the result. Try not to think about succeeding or failing. The only thing you should focus on is to have fun. The exercise is to, during the next ten days, to try something new or something that you know you are not good at. Each day, you should do at least one thing that challenges yourself. It doesn't have to be anything big. The most important thing is that you do it every day for at least ten days.

TIPS AND IDEAS ON THINGS YOU CAN TRY

* Are you bad at cooking, challenge yourself to cook.
* Have you always wanted to write, sit down and just write.
* Do you want to paint a picture but you are not so good at it, do it anyway.
* Want to learn a new sport, try it and see what you think.

It can be anything and it doesn't need to be the same thing every day. Write down what you're going to do and get started! And as I said: don't think in terms of success or failure. The only thing you should do in the coming days is to try to do something that seems interesting and have fun in the meantime. Who knows, you might find some new interests that you will love.

WHAT'S ON YOUR BUCKET LIST?

"Life is not measured by the number of breaths we take, but by the moments that take our breath away."

/ Unknown

"Life is short." "The days go by so fast." "Where did the time go?" Expressions people are using every day to describe how our life has passed. And certainly it's true that time goes by quickly. Life looks different to every one of us. Unfortunately, many live a life where you spend most of your time working. Hopefully we are working with something that we enjoy and that gives us many opportunities. In the worst case, we work long hours for a very low wage. When we get home we are tired, we lie down on the couch, watch some TV and go to sleep. History repeats itself day after day. If we have it good financially, we can live well, eat well and go on holidays. But it doesn't look like that for everyone. No matter how you live today, you have the chance to change your life and create more joy and spend your time in a better way.

BUCKET LIST, A NUMBER OF EXPERIENCES OR ACHIEVEMENTS THAT A PERSON HOPES TO HAVE OR ACCOMPLISH DURING THEIR LIFETIME.

The movie *The Bucket List* (2007, with among others, Jack Nicholson and Morgan Freeman) is about two older men who after a long life have become ill. They share a room in the hospital and that's where their friendship begins. Since they are going to die soon, they decide to make a list of the things that they want to experience and venture out into the wide world to fulfill some of the dreams before they take their last breath.

No matter how old we are, most of us have some things that we want to do in our lifetime. It's time to take charge over them now! Who knows what will happen tomorrow. What do you want to do and experience in your life?

THE DAY THAT NEVER COMES

There is a day that many of us are waiting for. You know that perfect day when the sun is shining and all the prerequisites to do what you long desired are perfect. Has that day arrived yet?

For most people, that perfect day when everything is just right will never happen. Therefore, it's time to start now. Wherever we find ourselves today, we can with small daily steps take us exactly where we want to go by starting now.

Soon, it's time to learn more about how you can influence your life in different areas: health, money, personality, relationships and socially. But first we are going to play and have some fun. You'll get to do your very own bucket list. Without any limitations in terms of time, money or opportunities you should write down exactly what you want to do before it's time for you to throw in the towel. And even if it feels scary to talk about death, it's actually the only thing that we cannot escape. We don't know when, but we know that everyone will die someday. Despite this, most of us live as if we would live forever. The samurai looked at death in a different way than we do today. Since they went to battle every day, they had to deal with the idea of death and live their lives accordingly. Every morning the samurai woke early, shaved and bathed. He put on clean clothes (kimono) and sharpened his sword. Before he left his home he bid farewell to his family in a dignified manner. In this way, he didn't fear death.

In a famous Japanese book, Hagakure, written by the great samurai Yamamoto Tsunetomo in the 1700's, it says:

"If by setting one's heart right every morning and evening, it's possible to live as though his body was already dead, he can feel freedom. His whole life will be without blame and he will succeed in his calling."

Although this is far from the reality we live in today, we can in many ways learn from the old samurai. By making the most of every day we have on earth, we can improve our quality of life and become better human beings.

But now it's enough about death, let's focus on life and play a little. We will play with the idea of what we would do with our lives if there were no limits. What places do you want to visit? What adventures would you carry out? Who would you like to meet? What do you want to buy? What do you want to give away?

Before you make your own bucket list, you can get some inspiration from mine. I'm working on it constantly and as soon as I come up with something I like to do, I write it down. To have a bucket list reminds me that life is indeed full of opportunities. When I have a good day I get inspired by looking at my list and get ideas on how I will be able to experience these things. But just like any other person, I sometimes wake up on the wrong side and by looking at my list, I immediately feel happier and uplifted.

THIS IS HOW MY BUCKET LIST LOOKS LIKE RIGHT NOW

- ✓ Watch the UFC in Las Vegas
- ✓ Swim and play with wild dolphins
- ✓ Safari in Africa, see wild lions, zebras and giraffes
- ✓ Travel to the Caribbean islands
- ✓ Travel to Antarctica and see wild penguins and polar bears
- ✓ Travel to Fiji

✓ Go to Nepal to hike and meditate

✓ Earn $10,000 in one day

✓ Experience the carnival in Rio de Janeiro

✓ Speak in front of 10,000 people

✓ Participate in a film

✓ Become such a good surfer so that I can handle a tube (surf through a wave)

✓ Touch the Hollywood sign

✓ Help a person to a better life

✓ Visit Okinawa with my father

✓ Move to LA

✓ Have a good relationship with my sister

✓ Do something great for my mom

✓ Drive a Lamborghini Gallardo

✓ Parachute

✓ Earn money while I sleep

✓ Bungee jump off a bridge in New Zealand (which goes straight down into a gorge)

✓ Hike to Pelisterski Oci, Macedonia (one of Macedonia's highest mountain and nature reserve)

✓ Save a life

Doesn't it sound fun? Hopefully you now feel inspired to make your own bucket list.

TASK

MAKE YOUR OWN BUCKET LIST

* Write down everything you want to do or experience before it's time to kick the bucket. Have fun and play with it. No wish is too small or too big. Don't think: "But I will never be able to do this, I can't..."Go for it and write down everything you would do if there were no limitations whatsoever.

ℓℓ ☆ ℓℓ

FOR MOST PEOPLE THE PERFECT DAY

*when everything is just right
will never happen.
Therefore, it's time
to start now.*

HEALTH GOALS

"Everything in moderation, nothing in excess."

/ Greek philosopher

The old quote above, "everything in moderation, nothing in excess", fits well with your health. I'm not a doctor but I do know that too much of anything is never good whether it be food, exercise or sleep. In this chapter you will learn a little more about how you can influence your health for the better. If you've already found a comfortable and healthy lifestyle: keep up the good work. But remember that health is a perishable thing and by reading the following pages, I'm convinced that you can find some great tips that will make your life healthier. Do you have problems with your health or feel like you don't have time to take care of yourself, you'll find a lot of useful information here. There is something for everyone, maybe it will be an awakening for you, a reminder, or anything in between. You will get to learn more about what is important for your physical and mental health, diet and sleep. And when you're done with this chapter, it's time to start your new, healthier life.

THE WOMAN WHO NEVER HAD TIME

Jennifer is a young career woman with her whole life ahead of her. After taking her law degree at Yale Law School she moved to Manhattan, New York to begin the journey towards becoming a successful lawyer. She loved to learn the profession. Every day she researched and studied old cases to find new approaches to her argumentation. Jennifer, who came from a hardworking family where your career was important, knew that in order to cope with a tough career it was very important to take care of your body, take breaks, eat healthy and get at least six to seven hours of sleep. At first things went well for Jennifer and she took the time to exercise, eat well, socialize with friends occasionally and get enough sleep.

Time passed and Jennifer became increasingly skilled at her profession. Soon, she was one of Manhattans most sought-after defense lawyers and she lined up one successful case after another. The more accomplished Jennifer became, the less time she had to take care of herself. She stopped exercising, slept less and ate more and more junk food. A few years later Jennifer, who still was a successful lawyer, had gained 50 pounds and she often felt tired and drained. Not to mention stressed. Jennifer had no time for anything other than her job. Christmas came and Jennifer went back home to her parents to celebrate the holidays and spend time with her family. As she walked through the door of her childhood home, her own mother didn't even recognize her. Apart from the fact that she had gained weight, her mother didn't see that joy of life that Jennifer had always had. Her happy face had been replaced by a face with bags under the eyes and an indifferent expression. Jennifer's mother had also been a successful and assertive business woman and during her 30 years as a business owner she always had a little picture on the desk that read: "Success without happiness and health is not success."

The next day Jennifer's mother cooked a delightful breakfast, she baked her special scones, cut up fresh tomatoes and cucumbers. She took out the cheese and marmalade and made some nice green tea. She even made fresh juice of oranges and a lemon in the blender that Jennifer had sent them for Christmas last year since she had been too busy to come home. Meanwhile, Jennifer was in her childhood bed and slept well.

She dreamed of her wonderful childhood and about the good times before the seriousness had started. She woke up well rested to the smell of freshly baked scones and went down the spiral staircase to the kitchen. During the next few hours, mother and daughter sat and talked about life. Jennifer explained how she didn't have time for anything and how she had lost the joy of life. The only thing that existed in her life was her career, the rest was a disaster. The mother who understood that the situation was serious, told Jennifer that it was time for her to choose a path in life. Either she could continue to live this way and her health and quality of life would only get worse and worse or she could choose to make a change and create a healthy life.

Naturally, Jennifer wanted to find happiness again but it had gone so far that she didn't know how she would get out of the rat race, which she herself had created.

During the next few days, the family celebrated a lovely Christmas with a lot of happiness, great food, rest and some skiing. Then the day came when it was time for Jennifer to go back to New York.

"Have you decided how you want to live the rest of your life?" asked Jennifer's mother.

Jennifer said that she had given it a lot of thought and decided that it was time for change. She would put her foot down. Certainly, she would continue with her work but she would make sure to prioritize her health and well-being. She would take on fewer cases and do them with greater enthusiasm. She would hire a talented apprentice who could do the basic research work.

Jennifer promised to get in touch with her old friends that she had lost touch with. She also promised herself to work out and eat healthy and sleep at least six to seven hours per night. When Jennifer's mother hugged and said goodbye to her daughter she felt that those days had made a difference and she was proud of her. When Jennifer came home that evening and unpacked her suitcase, she found a small package. She opened it and found the old worn picture with the text "Success without happiness and health is not success." On the back of the picture it read: "Never forget to take care of yourself and have fun Jennifer. I love you. / Your dear mother."

PHYSICAL EXERCISE

Physical exercise means that you move your body and hopefully have fun while doing it. Your body has to move every day to function, your heart needs to be engaged, the lungs have to work and so does your muscles. There are many different ways to exercise in order to feel good and here you will receive some tips. If you are a person who already exercise a lot, you might find some ideas to take your exercise to the next level.

Going to the gym is currently very popular or at least being a member of a gym. Perhaps you recognize yourself? Many obtain a gym membership without the knowledge or interest in that particular type of exercise. It's important to remember that there are many other ways to exercise than going to the gym, go for a light run or power walk.

Before we talk about how you can find a way to exercise that suits you, think about how your everyday life looks. If you have a physical job it's great, if you sit still all day long make sure to make your day more active. Take the opportunity to move around when you can, take the stairs instead of the elevator, go for a walk at lunch and why not park the car a few extra blocks from work. By moving around, you improve your health.

To find a form of exercise that suits you, it's important that you think it's fun, challenging, and that it gives you something in return. Remember that exercise can be anything: dance,

✺

TAKE THE OPPORTUNITY TO MOVE AROUND WHEN YOU CAN.

Take the stairs instead of the elevator, go for a walk at lunch and why not park the car a few extra blocks from work.
By moving around, you improve your health.

soccer, martial arts, gymnastics, running, shooting, skiing, motocross, surfing and a lot of other things. If you prefer to be on your own and are disciplined, you can take on your exercise by yourself and hire a trainer if necessary. If you tend to skip your exercise and like to meet people, I suggest that you exercise together with friends or become a member of an association or a club. USA has one of the world's widest range of activities and there are many activities to choose from. By joining an association or club, you get a trainer, you get the opportunity to meet new friends and you get an extra push to actually go there. If you exercise together with others and with a good instructor, you wouldn't want to miss out on the fun even if you are a bit tired after the events of the day.

For those of you who exercise regularly or at a high level, it's important that you dare to try new things and find new ways to develop to make your workout fun, challenging and rewarding. Why not go on a training camp, buy a new book about exercising or hire a personal trainer?

TIPS FOR YOUR EXERCISE
 * Find something you enjoy doing.
 * Ensure that the exercise is challenging and rewarding.
 * Exercise together with others.
 * Dare to try something new.
 * If you find it boring to go to the gym, find something else that suits you better. Exercising is everything that has to do with movement.

There have been plenty of research on how physical activity affects your health and well-being. It has been concluded that daily physical activity makes you feel better both physically and mentally. Additionally, research shows that the quality of your life increases and in many cases even your life span.

For those who actively exercise no research is required for

you to understand this, you know how good it feels to work out, especially afterwards. For those who are not actively exercising today, give yourself a chance to increase your well-being – you will not regret it.

Now you may be wondering how often, how hard, and how much you should exercise? It all depends on what your goals are with your workout. The amount of exercise and intensity varies considerably between a jogger and an elite athlete. Once you have set your goals, it's important that you get help from a personal trainer or a friend who knows about exercise.

Some general tips for those who are not yet very active are:

* Move your body for at least 30 minutes daily.
* At least twice a week, you should perform some form of physical activity, where you get to work hard and increase your heart rate – that is being short of breath. This type of exercise should be performed for at least 45 consecutive minutes.
* Find appropriate leisure activities where you do something you enjoy simultaneously as you move around.

MENTAL TRAINING

"If you continue to do what you've always done, you will get the same results you have always gotten."

/ Anthony Robbins

Did you know that a human thinks about 65,000 thoughts per day? 95 percent of those thoughts are the same as you thought yesterday. It means that if you don't change the way you think it will be hard to make a change. On the other hand: if you learn to master your thoughts and think the thoughts that are right for you, you will enter the right track. This is one of the reasons that a person can win again and again and succeed more and more. In sports, it's often not a very big difference between first, second and third place. How can it then be that the same person usually wins? Well, it depends on the mental training and thoughts.

Ingemar Stenmark, one of Sweden's greatest athletes and one of the world's most accomplished skiers, claimed that he never practiced mental training. Until one day when he attended a lecture about it. After the lecture, he reportedly said: "That's what I've always done." It's important that you learn to think the right thoughts. Since you are reading this book and have decided to develop yourself it means that you are concerned about your life and your thoughts. Maybe you're just like Stenmark, a person who naturally is mentally strong. If so, congratulations! But if you are like me and many others it might not feel that natural. In that case you will get some help from this book on how you can work with your way of thinking.

There are hundreds of different ways to work on the way you think, the most important thing is that it works for you. Generally, it's about having the ability to influence your thoughts in the direction you want. It's about visualizing your goals, which means seeing yourself achieving your goals in your head. The beautiful thing with your mind is that if you can imagine how you achieve a goal the brain perceives it as reality and gives you the confidence to do the same in reality. If you are interested in finding out more about mental training, I recommend you to go to Amazon.com or your local bookstore to find more in-depth books about mental training.

EXERCISE

Get a pen and paper and do the following exercise. Do it now! Keep working on this for at least ten days. It will help you to achieve your goals in the future and create a healthier and more balanced life.

* Write down three recurring thoughts that you want to change. For example: "I can't. It's not possible. I don't deserve this."
* Write down three positive thoughts that you should replace your old negative thoughts with. For example: "I can! It's possible! I deserve this!"
* The next time you have negative thoughts, say the word "STOP" to yourself and imagine a stop sign.
* Replace the old negative thought by saying a new positive thought to yourself at least three times.
* Repeat this every time a negative thought occurs.

In this way, you slowly but surely change your negative thoughts into something good and positive that brings you ahead in life. Although it's important to have patience. It won't work immediately, but by doing your homework, you will eventually have trained your mind to think the thoughts that enhances your quality of life and brings you closer to your goals.

Another exercise for you who ponders a lot is to once again get a pen and paper. Write down your thoughts, no matter how ugly and weird they are. Write down everything you think and feel for about 20 minutes. Both positive and negative. Don't judge the thoughts, just write them down.

When you're done, go through what you have written. The thoughts you don't like, you cross over. Before you finish this exercise, read the thoughts that are left (those that are not crossed out) three times.

For those of you who are new to working with yourself these exercises may feel strange at first, but do them with an open mind and give it a fair chance and you will see the benefit it has for your mind.

DIET

325 miles south of Japan's southernmost point, you will find the small island of Okinawa. In addition to its stunning white beaches, Okinawa is best known as the birthplace of karate. This is where karate developed before it spread to mainland Japan and later around the world. Okinawa also has the largest number of centenarians (a person who lives to or beyond the age of 100 years) in the world. Much research has been done on the subject and the diet of people in Okinawa is said to be one of the major factors that they grow so old. In addition to a healthy diet, it's said that another big reason that life expectancy is so high is the fact that elderly are well-respected in the community and take part in young people's activities and events.

How do Okinawans eat to get so old? Well, they eat by the motto Hara Hachi Bu, which means "stop eating when you feel full to 80 percent." In addition, they eat a very nutritious and plant-based diet rich in antioxidants and low in calories.

EXAMPLES OF HEALTHY FOOD FROM OKINAWA
* Vegetables
* Root vegetables
* Fruit
* Tofu
* Wholegrain
* Legumes
* Fish

Surveys show that Okinawans, by staying active and eating a healthy diet where they stop eating when they feel full to 80 percent, creates several positive consequences. Except that they live long, studies show that cardiovascular diseases and certain forms of cancers (including breast and prostate cancer) are much lower than in the US, for example.

Perhaps this type of diet is something for you? When it comes to diets there are many experts and many philosophies that tells you what's right and wrong. The important thing for you is not getting confused in this existing jungle. What you must remember is that if you want to live a successful and happy life you need energy and one of the biggest contributing factors to this is to eat a good, healthy diet. Now you may wonder if that means that you never can wolf down a pizza, some beer, popcorn, chips and maybe some candy? You remember the motto "everything in moderation, nothing in excess"? As long as you eat healthy and nutritious food most of the time it's okay to occasionally "cheat".

I cannot tell you exactly how you should eat, but I will give you some tips that hopefully will increase your awareness of your diet. If you follow them, you will probably feel better and have more energy. The energy you need to live the life you wish to live!

HOW MANY TIMES A DAY SHOULD I EAT?
Breakfast, lunch, dinner, and two to three smaller snacks.

BREAKFAST TIPS
Oatmeal, eggs, whole wheat bread, crisp bread, turkey, fruit and more.

LUNCH AND DINNER TIPS
Half of your plate consists of salad, a quarter of carbs (pasta, potatoes, rice, etc.), and a quarter of chicken, fish or meat. Dare to vary your salad with nutritious vegetables such as cucumber, tomato, lettuce, avocado, spinach, carrots, radishes and onions. Olive oil, vegeta and plenty of lemon in the salad makes it a wonderful flavor experience.

SNACK TIPS
Fruit, cottage cheese, crisp bread with turkey, nuts, avocados, eggs.

Avoid: Fast food, processed and frozen prepackaged meals.

ꙮ ☆ ꙮ

TAKE A HOT BATH, READ A BOOK OR JUST RELAX.

Dim the lights and reduce the noise level.

Avoid activities such as working, paying bills, or solving family problems before bedtime.

You should eat cooked food at least once a day. Remember that it's you who decide how the food should be. By having a little imagination you can eat really good food that also is healthy. If you don't know much about food and nutrition ask someone around you who knows, take a cooking class or buy a book on healthy food.

Also, try to take the time to eat together with your loved ones at least once a day. Sit down and eat in peace and quiet, talk, socialize and have fun. The dinner is a natural gathering place, be sure to take advantage of it instead of eating while watching TV or playing with your smartphone. Good luck!

SLEEP

Do you sleep well at night? From the mid-1990s until the late 2000s, the number of people with sleeping problems have doubled. Younger adults, teenagers and women are among the worst affected. Some of the most common reasons are: worry about not being able to sleep, worry about something important in life and irregular bedtimes. In the following paragraph you will learn a little more about sleep and what you can do to sleep better.

Just like with most other things, sleep works differently for everyone and if you've found a strategy that feels good to you, just continue on the same track. But you can forget one thing, the myth that you should get 8 hours of sleep every night.

First of all, new research shows that the need for eight hours of uninterrupted sleep is a myth. According to historian A. Roger Ekirch of Virginia Tech, the sleeping pattern was completely different until the end of the 1600s, as one slept in two periods. First they went to bed, slept for four hours and then woke to occupy themselves with something. One to two hours later they slept for about another four hours. During waking hours at night ordinary activities were: sex, going to the toilet, smoking, writing or visiting the neighbors. As you're reading this book, and have decided on a change in your life, your sleeping habits will probably also change. Your work with written goals leads to you taking care of yourself to have the strength to do your homework and work towards your goals every day. The result is that you sleep better, not necessarily more. I don't know how much you sleep today, but expect that you will get six, seven hours of sleep per night. And the fact is that it's more than enough if you sleep well during these hours. Also: when you are starting to have a meaning with your life you are a person with a plan. You have things to do and look forward to: places to be, people to meet and adventures to create. Think back to those evenings when you went to bed knowing that the next day you had a date or job interview or going away on a trip you have long dreamed of. Is it hard to get up in the morning even though you haven't slept eight hours?

When you have a meaning with your life it's easier to get up in the morning. Certainly, there will be days when you rather want to hide under the covers, but your goals will help you to get up from bed.

SEVEN TIPS FOR BETTER SLEEP

1. Take a hot bath, read a book or just relax. Dim the lights and reduce the noise level. Avoid activities such as working, paying bills, or solving family problems before bedtime.
2. Try to go to bed and get up at about the same time each day.
3. Create a soothing atmosphere in your bedroom. A dark, cool and quiet room will help you sleep better.
4. Invest in a good bed and pillows, after all you spend a lot of time of your life here.

5. Avoid caffeine five, six hours before bedtime. Caffeine is found in, among other things, coffee, tea, soda and chocolate.

6. Hopefully you don't smoke. If you do, avoid cigarettes a couple of hours before bedtime. Nicotine can cause difficulty falling asleep, difficulty waking in the morning and even nightmares.

7. Avoid alcohol. Although many see alcohol as relaxing it actually disrupts your sleep. Drinking alcohol before bed leads to a night of poorer sleep.

YOUR HEALTH GOALS

Now it's finally time for you to set your first real goal, take charge of your future and create the life you want. Your health is perhaps the most important in order for you to be able to live a good life. Imagine if you had everything you ever wanted, but at the same time was very sick. Would you then be able to enjoy your success, your money or your relationships? Now is the time to set goals and make a plan for how you want to take care of your body and your mind. You choose what you want to improve with your health. It can be to quit smoking, eat healthier or lose weight. Maybe all three. For those of you who feel that you are good at exercising, but sleep too little perhaps it's time to start working on your routines before bedtime. That's enough talking and time for action. Straighten up, take a deep breath and get started with the following exercises. Don't start tomorrow or in a week, start now!

TASK: HEALTH GOALS

1. Your first task is to write down everything you want to improve with your health. It can be anything and how much as you want. Dare to write down exactly what you would like to achieve: how you want to exercise, how you want your body to look, how you want to feel, how you want to eat, how you

want to think, how you want to wake up in the morning, how you want to feel after a day at work and more. Don't set any limits and don't think about how you will achieve it.

EXAMPLE

- » I want to quit smoking.
- » I want to lose 20 pounds.
- » I want to sleep well at night and wake up feeling refreshed.
- » I want to think positive thoughts about myself.
- » I want to see the world with positive eyes.
- » I want to find a fun way to exercise.
- » I want to learn how to cook healthy and tasty food.

2. **Read through** what you have written and choose the three most important goals you have written down.

3. **With a couple of sentences**, write down what it will mean to you when you succeed in achieving your three most important goals.

EXAMPLE

QUIT SMOKING

Quitting smoking would mean that I feel much better and increase my chances of living longer. It would also make me save money and a lot of time I spend on standing around smoking.

LOSE 20 POUNDS

By losing 20 pounds I can get rid of the love handles around my waistline. I will feel more attractive and feel better. My health will improve and to maintain my new weight I will eat and live healthier, which in turn will lead to a healthier body.

LEARN HOW TO COOK HEALTHY AND TASTY FOOD

By learning how to cook healthy and tasty food, I will be able to take responsibility for eating good and nutritious food. It will give me more energy and will make me feel better.

4. Now you have figured out three things that you want to improve with your health. You have also written down what it would mean to achieve your goals. Before we make a plan for how to achieve the goals, we need to set a time limit. Remember that a goal without a time limit is not a goal. Carefully consider how long it will take to achieve your goals. It's important that you set a deadline that feels reasonable, it cannot be so short that you feel you are not capable of it. On the other hand, it cannot be so far away that you forget the goals.

EXAMPLE

Goal 1: Stop smoking.
Time Limit: Six months.

Goal 2: Lose 20 pounds.
Time Limit: Three months.

Goal 3: Learn how to cook healthy and tasty food.
Time Limit: Six months.

The time limit for goals can be anything from one day to several years, it depends entirely on what type of goal it is. Sometimes it can be difficult to estimate how long it will take to reach a goal. If you are unsure, it's important that you ask yourself the question: "What do I need to do to achieve this goal?" By your answer, you can better determine what deadline to set for your goals.

Good job. You have now written down your goals, and what it will mean to you when you achieve them and when to achieve them. Here comes the most important thing: to make a plan for how you will achieve them. The plan includes subgoals and activities required to achieve your goal.

Simply put, it's now that you will write down what you need to do every day, every week or every month to achieve your goal. You can add a reward for when you achieve your sub-goals, which gives you something extra to fight for.

A good tip is to distribute the activities evenly within your time limit. If your goal is to do 1000 push-ups in ten weeks you can easily figure out your sub-goals, which is how many push-ups to do per week: 100 (1000 pushups/10 weeks = 100 pushups/week). All goals are not this easy to divide, but be creative – it's your life we are talking about. And you know what: it will be worth it!

EXAMPLE

Goal: Lose 20 pounds.
Time Limit: Three months

SUCCESS PLAN

Activities: Hire a personal trainer. Follow the exercise and diet plan.

Sub-goal 1: After one month, I will have lost at least seven pounds.
Reward: A nice dinner with the family.

Sub-goal 2: After the second month, I will have lost at least fourteen pounds.
Reward: A day at the spa with massage.

Ultimate Goal: After three months, I have lost twenty pounds.
Reward: A fit body and a healthy lifestyle.

The plan is to follow my personal trainer's exercise and diet plan to one hundred percent. By being disciplined and doing that, I will achieve my goal.

This is your first plan. How does it feel? A little nervous maybe. Remember that just by writing down these three health goals, you are on the right path. Remember the study of Harvard students and how richly rewarded they became?

Now comes the most important thing: to actually dare to go after your goals. You will be greatly rewarded with improved health and an enhanced quality of life.

Good luck with your health goals!

MONEY GOALS

"Money may not buy happiness, but I'd rather cry in a Jaguar than on a bus."

/ Françoise Sagan

Money, money, money. Many people are fascinated by money and wealth, others despise money and say it's the work of the devil. What is your attitude towards money? Do you wish you were rich and could buy whatever you want or are you satisfied with your finances as it is today? Managed properly, money is something good, it can give you the freedom to create the life you desire, it can give you the opportunity to travel and adventure, it can give you a nice home or education for you and your children. Money can give you the opportunity to help other people, it can give you the freedom to do whatever you want in your life.

We have been taught that it's important to get a good education so that we can get a good job that is secure and well-paid. We are studying a lot of mathematics, chemistry, physics, physical education, history, English and so on. But what the school system and the community often fail to teach us is how we earn money and manage them so that they grow. We are told that it's important to save but place our money in a regular bank account, with hardly any interest at all, instead of investing and letting the money grow. We learn to work for money instead of learning how money works for us.

In this chapter, you will learn more about money, so you can do more things that you long to do. You will get tips on how you can earn more money and save more while you're living a better life. You will learn what to do to get your money working for you and how you can create a life where money is not a problem. Last but not least you will be making your own plan for your financial dreams. A great change awaits you and if you are willing to work for it, I promise you a reward is just around the corner.

Although money itself is not the ultimate goal, they represent freedom, the freedom to do things. To have enough capital makes it possible to enjoy the best experiences and products the world has to offer.

THE RICHEST MAN IN BABYLON

Already in 1926, George S. Clason wrote the book *The Richest Man in Babylon*. If you haven't already read it, I highly recommend that you do so. A lot of advice that you currently receive regarding money originates from that particular book. It's about Babylon, which in ancient times was the richest city in the world. By applying simple principles to acquire, retain and get their money to grow, the residents of Babylon succeeded in becoming rich. The principles were simple but worked very well. When it comes to acquiring money and become rich, there are no shortcuts, it's required that you use your time to learn about money and how to get them to grow.

In Babylon they developed seven cures for a lean purse. By applying them, you can also make sure that your wallet grows.

The seven cures are:

1. PAY YOURSELF FIRST

The key principle to generate wealth is to pay yourself first. The principle is simple: save at least one-tenth of what you earn. By saving a tenth of what you earn and investing the money it will eventually grow into a fortune (more on this later). Many live month to month and when pay day is approaching the account is starting to get empty. Therefore, it's important to put aside at least one-tenth every time you get paid.

2. CONTROL YOUR EXPENSES

In today's society where it's easy to buy on credit and lend money, many of us spend more than we earn. It means that every month we have a negative balance. Make sure to reduce your expenses so that you spend less than you earn and put aside at least one-tenth of your income.

3. GET YOUR GOLD TO MULTIPLY

It's important that you learn how to invest to get your money to grow. Once you become disciplined enough to save a tenth of everything you earn and you can control your spending, it's time to learn how to invest your money. By understanding compound interest (more on this later) your money will grow into a fortune.

4. GUARD YOUR TREASURE WELL

As your wealth grows, investment offers will increase. If it sounds too good to be true, it probably is. By not being tempted to take any shortcut to wealth and instead invest safely with good returns, your assets will grow slowly but surely without risk of being lost.

5. MAKE YOUR HOME A PROFITABLE INVESTMENT

Just like many today recommend you to buy your property, the inhabitants of Babylon also got the same advice. By taking a portion of your income and invest it in a home, you and your family will have a nice place to live while your chances of getting rich increases. Many people who bought a property at the

ᥬᥬ ☆ ᥬᥬ

THE KEY PRINCIPLE TO

*generate wealth
is to pay yourself first.*

right price has seen it increase a lot in value. If you furthermore can turn your house into a rental property, you will also get a monthly income from your tenants.

6. ENSURE A FUTURE INCOME

This principle is about making yourself ready for the days when you can no longer work. By starting to save and invest in a timely manner along with paying off the loan on your property, you can secure the wealth for you and your family until you get old.

7. INCREASE YOUR EARNING POWER

The final cure for an empty wallet is all about increasing your ability to earn money. By constantly learning more about things and having a good work ethic, you will be better equipped to make more money. Wealth begins in small amounts to gradually become larger.

Last but not least, the rich men of Babylon preached that it's important to pay off your debts. Two-tenths of your income would be used to pay off your loan until you were debt free, one-tenth would be saved and you would manage to live on the remaining seven tenths of your income.

These tips, which is thus written in the 1920s, is the basis of all financial advice we have today. They are practical and simple but most importantly, they actually work.

Imagine that you earn \$3,000 per month after tax. How much would you be able to save if you put aside one-tenth of it, that is \$300 (3000/10 = \$300) per month?

After 1 year:	\$3,600
After 5 years:	\$18,000
After 10 years:	\$36,000
After 20 years:	\$72,000

As you can see it grows to a lot of money. In this example, you have only saved your money in a regular bank account without interest. You will later in this chapter learn more about the effects of compound interest and how it will make your money grow significantly faster.

HOW TO MAKE YOUR MONEY LAST LONGER

There are two ways to have more money left at the end of the month. One is to spend less money and the other is to earn more. For many of us, it sounds boring to spend less money. "But I want to treat myself to what I want, that's why I work," you might think. Obviously, it's important to indulge in the pleasures that life has to offer, but there are ways to actually save without cutting back on what you want. With a little planning and price comparisons you can get more money left over.

The first and most important tip for saving money is to look over your electricity bills, insurance and phone plans. Only here, there are several hundreds to save. Additionally, you should compare the prices of the grocery stores where you shop. Many grocery stores have a few inexpensive items, to lure you in, then they charge extra for everything else. Compare the products you buy frequently to see which supermarket is the cheapest. Ensure to buy in bulk a few times a month instead of going to the grocery store every day, so you save both gas and money while minimizing your impulsive purchases.

If you want to save even more, a good tip is to start taking a lunch box to work. Instead of paying $10 to $15 every day for lunch at a restaurant, you can bring your own tasty food. If you eat lunch out twice a week instead of five, you save about $1,500 a year. Money you can use for other more fun things. Also, look over your mortgage and credit – perhaps you can negotiate the interest rates or switch to a bank with better conditions.

EXERCISE

To gain more understanding of what you do with your money, you should write down every purchase you make for one month. Everything from chewing gum from the gas station to paying your rent.

DIVIDE YOUR BUDGET INTO THE FOLLOWING ACCOUNTS:

» Accommodation
» Food
» Transportation
» Clothes
» Savings
» Other
» Loans

After one month, you can clearly see what you have spent your money on. Look into where your money goes and think about how you want to spend it in the future.

THE ART OF EARNING MORE

In order to earn a lot of money, it's important that you're not afraid to work, it's also important that you learn to take care of the money you actually have. As we have already noted, there are two ways to acquire more money: either by spending less or earn more. Although it's important to review your costs and know what you spend money on, I prefer the latter option. It's always fun to earn more money.

The attitude you have when it comes to earning or spending money is very important. Either you can say: "I cannot afford it!" Or you can say, "What should I do to afford it?" This is very well described in the book Rich Dad, Poor Dad by Robert Kiyosaki.

If you want to live a life where money is no problem, it's time that you ask yourself the question: "What should I do to afford it?" Your brain will then begin to work and give you ideas. Ideas that you can develop and start making money on.

There are many, many ways to earn more money, it's only your imagination that sets the limits. In the following paragraph, you will get a few tips from me that can increase the size of your wallet.

Perhaps the easiest way is to take a second job. Only by working, for example, one Saturday a month, you can get a few extra hundred dollars that you can use for you and your family as well as your savings.

Another good tip is to review the possibility of switching to a job where you get paid better. You can also talk to your employer and tell them that you want to develop and ask what would be required of you in order to be promoted to another position with a higher salary. Yet another way to cash in money is to clean the garage and sell your old stuff at the local market, in your neighborhood or on Ebay. Did you know that the average person has unused items worth about $3,000 in their homes? If you run your own business or working as a salesman on commission, you can cash in a lot more money by contacting more companies, offer a greater solution or develop your way of selling.

As I said, there are thousands of ways for you to earn more money, if you are a little creative and not afraid to work. By creating an additional income or increasing your current income, you can also increase the quality of your life and treat yourself to that "little extra" that you dream of.

EXERCISE

Write down at least five things you could do to earn more money today. Note! Do the exercise now, not tonight, tomorrow or the next week.

SAVINGS

Although the term "American Dream" is used in many ways its essential idea is that anyone in the US through hard work has the potential to live a happy, meaningful and successful life. But what does the American Dream mean today? In a survey conducted 2014 by PolicyInteractive for the Center for a New American Dream they found what was most important in todays Americans' vision for the "Amercian Dream". The survey showed that the Americans number one dream was having personal freedom (78%), followed by the dream of having their basic needs met (75%) and achieving one's potential (71%). The dream of personal freedom contains health, financial freedom (being debt free and live a good life without having to worry about money) and the ability to control how you spend your time.

What you should ask yourself is what are you doing to attain this dream? By using the tools given in this book you can work your way to the life that you desire but it won't be enough to just read this book and think positive. I want to congratulate you on taking hold of your life and starting to read and work with this book. You have realized that dreams must be converted to a goal (remember: a goal is a written down dream with a deadline). The goals must be made to sub-goals and to succeed we need a plan. You have to follow your plan and take action everyday to attain that pot of gold at the end of the rainbow.

Without seeming pessimistic, it's important to understand that there are very few shortcuts to achieve your goals. To do what most people do is not going to take you to the life you desire. If you want to achieve something good, it's important that you write down your goals, make an activity plan, roll up your sleeves and start working. Day by day, step by step, you will succeed with whatever it is you want. This is how basically all successful people have done and they are not smarter than you in any way. The only difference between those who have succeeded from those who have not, is that they have done their homework every day.

The absolute best way to start building a fortune is to save monthly. Open a savings account that you cannot touch. Contact your bank and ask that they automatically transfer one tenth of your paycheck to your savings account as soon as the salary comes in. By paying yourself first, you make sure that you actually keep something from your earnings. Eventually there will be a lot of money by doing this.

If you take on a part-time job, my tip is to save half of what you earn in addition to your regular income. By doing that, you get the best of both worlds. Let's say you make $200 extra one month, then you save $100 and have a hundred left in your pocket to do something fun with. When money is starting to gather up, you will notice how much fun it is to actually have paid yourself. Just as I talked about earlier in the book balance is very important. By finding a balance in your finances, your wealth will grow. Also keep in mind the saying "Everything in moderation, nothing in excess", meaning that it's important not to save too much. For example, if you put aside 50 percent of your income and that leads to that you're not treating yourself to something extra and just eat cheap food, you will grow tired of it quickly. Chances are that you stop saving altogether. Small steps each day is the key to successful saving.

INVESTMENTS

An investment is easily explained as anything you put your money on and where you expect them to grow, meaning that you get a return. I don't know what level you are in terms of investments, but no matter where you are, here is some useful information that you could use to succeed with your investments in the future.

If you follow my advice, your savings will most likely increase in the coming years. Despite the fact that the US today have many highly paid and well-educated people, it's scary how little knowledge many have about investments. You rely completely on your banker, who often have a few hundreds of customers to take care of and provides general advice that aims to help you reach about the same return as the average.

There are several types of investments and I urge you to learn more about all of them to form your own opinion about what is good for you. By taking a stand, you increase your chances of success. The biggest mistake that many make is that they work hard, save a lot, but don't know anything about what they have invested in. If they're lucky it goes well, if they're unlucky they lose a lot of money. Leave nothing to chance, be sure to make good investments.

The investments I have concentrated on are shares and mutual funds. Shares mean, as you probably know, an investment in a company; when you buy shares, you buy shares in a company, that is, you become part owner. If the company does well and the market expects it to continue to do well, the shares increase in value.

Mutual funds are simply described as a collection of investments in shares and other securities as a trustee is in charge of who tries to manage them in the best way. The advantage of mutual funds is that you spread the risks and that there are experts that manages the fund. The fund can be a simple way to invest in companies from all over the world. For example, if you believe that growth will be large in Africa, there are so-called Africa funds.

There are tons of books on shares, mutual funds and retirement plans and I encourage you to read further on the subject to help you learn more about investing. One book that I particularly would like to recommend is *Money – Master the Game* by Tony Robbins. Before you invest in real life, you can make a portfolio where you shop with fictitious money. That way, you'll learn more about shares and funds without the risk of losing real money. You can make a portfolio on for example www.morningstar.com.

Historically, the US stock market (S&P 500) has on average provided a return of 10 percent since its inception 1928 through 2014. This means that if you during this period, had saved $300 a month for let's say 30 years, with 10 percent return you would have had approximately $620,000. That's not bad.

One thing that is important to take into account when you deal with shares and mutual funds is that there is always a risk of losing money.

SOME THINGS TO CONSIDER WHEN YOU INVEST IN MUTUAL FUNDS

» Save monthly – by buying funds each month you reduce the risk. When the stock market is low, you get more shares and your average rate decreases.

» Look up fees – it's important that you check the fees of the funds you invest in. For example, if you want to invest in a fund that follows the US stock market index (S&P 500), there are many equivalent funds. The difference is that some of them charge much higher fees than others. A 1.5 percent management fee may not sound like much but the fact is that 30 percent of the capital may be lost to the fund companies.

» Spread your risks – don't put all your eggs in one basket. Spread your investments to other countries and directions to reduce risk and increase the chances of getting it right.

» Invest for the long term – think long term of at least five years. By thinking long term your chances of receiving a good return increases. Historically, the stock market's return had large variations from year to year, but in the long term, the stock market has generated very good returns.

» Stay up to date – follow your funds and read about what is happening in the world. If there are major changes, consider switching investment strategy.

When it comes to investing in individual shares, it's important that you have a strategy and stay up to date with the stock market and what happens around the world. It's also important that you read about companies that you intend to invest in. One of the world's best investors is American Warren Buffett, who has created a fortune equivalent to over $60 billion dollars. Through perseverance, deliberation and insight he has managed to buy the right companies and in most cases retained his shares in them. Warren Buffett's investment company Berkshire Hathaway has on average had a return of 20 percent a year for the past 45 years.

WARREN BUFFETT'S TIPS FOR SUCCESSFUL STOCK INVESTING

» Think long term – plan to own your shares for many years.

» Understand what it is that you are buying. You need to understand the business idea of the company you invest in. Never trade anything you don't understand.

» Avoid any company that hopes for technological breakthroughs or where one is dependent on the skills of the employees.

» Know your companies well – it's better to have a small portfolio where you know what you are investing in than having a lot of companies where you don't know what they are doing.

» When you buy, buy a lot!

THE POWER OF COMPOUNDING

Albert Einstein called compound interest the eight wonder of the world. According to him, it was the most powerful force in the universe and the most important mathematical discovery ever.

One big reason that many people don't save is that they feel that it's impossible to become rich just by saving. The possibility to create financial freedom feels so hopeless that people instead spend all their money and buy a lottery ticket now and then, hoping to take a shortcut to wealth. Although I really hope you win on your lottery tickets, chances are minimal. The lottery companies are for-profit companies and exist due to the fact that most people lose on gambling, that's how they earn their money.

Did you know that by saving $500 per month, you can have $100,000 in ten years? For example: $500 x twelve months = $6,000 per year. $6,000 x ten years = $60,000. With the return that the US stock market (S&P 500) on average has generated since its inception 1928 (10 percent), your money will grow to $100,000 in about ten years. This is what's called the effect of compound interest, meaning that as your money grows, you also get a return on the money that has grown. Sounds complicated? Let's sort it out step-by-step.

EXAMPLE

Frank has invested $10,000 in funds that follow the US stock market (S&P 500). Every year the value grows with ten percent.

This is how Frank's principal amount develop during ten years:

Year 1: $10,000 x 1.1 (ten percent increase in value) = $11,000
Increase in value: $1,000

Year 2: 11,000 x 1.1 = $12,100
Increase in value: $1,100

Since Frank's money has grown the second year to $11,000 he will now get an increase in value of the new amount ($11,000). The increase in value grows every year as the money grows even if the percentage increase in value remains the same. This increases the annual return as the capital grows. Simply stated, it means that the more the money increases, the more money it generates.

Year 3: $12,100 x 1.1 = $13,310
Increase in value: $1,210

Year 4: $13,310 x 1.1 = $14,641
Increase in value: $1,331

Year 5: $14,641 x 1.1 = $16,105
Increase in value: $1,464

Year 6: $16,105 x 1.1 = $17,715
Increase in value: $1,610

Year 7: $17,715 x 1.1 = $19,486
Increase in value: $1,771

Year 8: $19,486 x 1.1 = $21,435
Increase in value: $1,949

Year 9: $21,435 x 1.1 = $23,578
Increase in value: $2,143

Year 10: $23,578 x 1.1 = $25,936
Increase in value: $2,358

Total growth over 10 years: $15,936 (25,936–10,000= $15,936)

In ten years, Frank has therefore more than doubled his $10,000 without really doing anything except having invested wisely in funds. By investing the right way in securities that grows, your money will be reproduced by the effect of compound interest. The longer you save, the greater the impact.

In the example, Frank didn't save monthly at all. How much more money do you think he would have received if he had saved $200 a month during those ten years?

Well, if Frank had saved $200 a month, in addition to the $10,000 which he invested in funds, his capital would have grown to more than $66,000. Just by making a small sacrifice, Frank could in ten years enjoy his capital grow to $66,000.

If Frank instead had saved for 20 years, the balance would have been more than $200,000. By learning how to invest well and learning more about the effect of compound interest you can also experience the increase in value of your money. The more time that passes, the thicker your wallet will become. On www.thecalculatorsite.com you can easily calculate the effect of compound interest. Remember to invest wisely only with money that you can afford to spare, past performance does not guarantee future results.

RULE OF 72

To make it easier for you to calculate the effect of compound interest there is a simple tool that you can use: the rule of 72.

By dividing the number 72 by the annual return, you can see how many years it will take for your money to double.

Example: Divide 72 by the expected return, in this case 8 percent. 72/8 = nine years.

It means that in nine years you double your principal amount if you get a return of eight percent per year and returns are reinvested.

Inversely, you can also easily figure out what return you need to double your capital at a certain time.

Example: You want to double your principal amount in six years. 72/6 = 12 percent. That means for you to double your investment in six years it will require an annual return of 12 percent.

ℰℰ ☆ ℰℰ

AN INVESTMENT IS EASILY EXPLAINED

as anything you put your money on and where you expect them to grow, meaning that you get a return.

In this way, you can easily start working with the effect of compound interest. My hope is that with this knowledge you now feel motivated to begin to earn more money, save more and invest well. I hope you're ready, because now is the time to set your first money goal!

TASK: MONEY GOALS

No matter what income you have, or what knowledge you possess when it comes to money, it's difficult to achieve something without written goals and plans. Remember that to be successful with your financial goals it's important to think long term and make a realistic plan that you can follow up and work with daily. Today, you will set three goals. The first goal is a financial goal that is about something you've always wanted. Now it's time to take control over it.

The second goal is about your monthly income, it's time for you to decide how big you want it to be and what you should do to get there. If you already have a high monthly income maybe your goal is about how you can work less and still earn the same amount. Remember that balance is important in life. Only through balance we can be truly happy and successful.

The third and perhaps most enjoyable goal, is how much you desire to have in assets in five to ten years.

When setting your goals, it's important that you ask yourself the question, "Why is this my goal?" or "What will it mean if I achieve this goal?" If you don't know why you want to achieve something, it becomes difficult to motivate you to keep going when it gets tough. Because it will get tough sometimes, if it were easy everyone would be millionaires. But if you're ready to have fun with this while you work daily making small advancements toward your goals you will have all the money you desire faster than you think. And with that money you can feel safe and create the life you want. A life full of adventure, joy and happiness.

This is the first activity that you can do today. This means that you're getting started right away to work towards your goals instead of procrastinating them.

» What do you want to do, experience or buy?
» Write down something that you have long dreamed of doing or buying. It could be a trip, a car, an experience or whatever you want to do but for some reason have postponed.
» Set a deadline to your goals.
» Make an action plan of what you need to do to succeed in achieving your goal. How much do you need to save each month? What do you need to find out? And so on.
» Set sub-goals.
» Write down an activity that you can do today.
» Get started, do your homework every day and enjoy the process!

EXAMPLE 1

Goal: Travel to my dream destination Italy.
Deadline: One year.
Activity plan:
» Buy a book on Italy to learn more about the country.
» Go online and research traveling options.
» Monthly savings: $300. Price of the trip: $3,600 (3600/12 =$300).

Sub-goal 1: to have saved at least $900 after three months.
Reward: Arrange an Italian evening at home with good Italian food and music.

Sub-goal 2: To have saved at least $1,800 after six months.
Reward: Visit our favorite Italian restaurant with my family.

Sub-goal 3: To have saved at least $2,700 after nine months.
Reward: Arrange an Italian pizza party with tasty pizza and delicious drinks.

Ultimate Goal: To have saved $3,600 after twelve months.
Reward: Departure to Italy.
Activity to do today: Go to the bookstore and buy a book on Italy and read at least 20 pages in it.

Don't forget to give yourself small rewards when you achieve your sub-goals. It makes the journey towards your ultimate goal much more fun.

EXAMPLE 2
Goal: Earn $5,000 per month.
Current situation: $3,500 per month.
Deadline: Three years.
Activity plan:
  » Educate myself to get promoted in my current job.
  » Schedule meetings with my manager to talk about my development in the company.
  » Look into whether it's time for me to switch to another company or if I should stay.
  » Start my own business for extra income. Start selling pajamas of organic cotton through my own e-commerce website. Look into what is required and learn more about e-commerce.

Ultimate Goal: Within three years, I have increased my monthly income to $5,000.
Reward: Buy a Chevrolet Camaro.
Activity to do today: Schedule a meeting with the manager to discuss my future at the company.

EXAMPLE 3
Goal: I want to have at least $100,000 within ten years.
Motivation: By working towards my financial goals, I will increase the joy and the possibilities for me, my family, friends

and other people. During the journey, I will experience challenges and successes that bring me and my surroundings many moments of joy and development. Last but not least, this financial goal will make it possible for me to live the life I want and at the same time help other people.

Current situation: $10,000 invested in US Index Funds.

Target return: 8 percent per year.

Monthly savings: $500. By counting the effect of compound interest on www.thecalculatorsite.com I have concluded that my assets will grow to over $100,000 in ten years if I get an average return of eight per cent per year and save $500 per month.

Deadline: Ten Years

Activity Plan:

Figure out if I can lower my expenses, increase my income, or perhaps both.

- » Learn more about investments and savings.
- » Look over my budget to follow my monthly savings.
- » Find a way to increase my monthly income through for example, a part-time job.
- » Set a target return for my savings.
- » See how the money is affected by compound interest
- » Stay up-to-date with my investments.
- » Spread my risks and follow the stock market's development.

Sub-goal 1: Within three years, I have $30,000.

Reward: Any entertainment for a value of $750.

Sub-goal 2: Within five years, I have $50,000.

Reward: Any entertainment for a value of $1,500.

Ultimate Goal: In ten years I will have $100,000.

Reward: A trip to Bora Bora for a value of $5,000.

Activity to do today: Set a new budget to make sure that I can save $500 per month.

You have now set your first financial goals, you have made an action plan and you have set sub-goals. Good job! If you're working towards these goals and not give up, you will achieve them, I'm convinced of that.

One thing that is important to think about when it comes to your goals, activities and sub-goals is to be flexible along the way. If your circumstances change, dare to change your goal and work according to your new conditions. Remember that just by being on the way to your new goals you can reach a lot further than if you wouldn't have started at all. Sometimes you will notice that something on the way doesn't work, then you have to quickly adjust and try something new.

And one last thing before we move on. Although it feels scary with these goals, you should know that it's not *rocket science* when it comes to creating a fortune. There are thousands of stories of people with circumstances similar to yours who have succeeded, if they can do it, you can. Go for it!

ᘒ ☆ ᘒ

PERSONAL GOALS

"The journey of a thousand miles begins with one step."

/ Lao Tzu

My goal for this book was to write every day between the hours of 10:00 am and 1.30 pm. I have decided to write at least two pages a day, no matter how difficult and tough it can be. Some days, I have written two pages in one hour and other days I had to continue to late afternoon or stop the writing to come back to it later in the day. Today is a day when one of my big goals have been met. Just before I left for the library, I received some great news that I've been waiting for: I will soon become self-employed. It's something I have long been waiting for and I look forward to my journey from novice to successful entrepreneur. Although I most of all would like to celebrate the news, 18 minutes later I sit here writing on my book. I will jot down my two pages and then I will celebrate with a good lunch with one of my dearest friends.

What do I mean by this? Well, it's important that you do your homework, even on days when you don't feel like it. Just like the old Chinese philosopher Lao Tzu said, "The journey of a thousand miles begins with one step." Everything begins with one small step and by taking one step at a time and constantly dare to move forward you will achieve what you wish for. Sometimes you will be sad and sometimes very happy, as

I am today. Some days you may not feel like working towards your goals, but it's precisely these days that it's most important to do so. Do you know who the boxer Muhammad Ali is? Muhammad Ali is one of history's greatest athletes and several times he became world champion in boxing's most prestigious weight class, heavy weight. Through his amazing boxing and sharp tongue, he managed to become an icon and inspiration to millions of people around the world. Muhammad Ali quickly understood that to succeed in anything in life you have to believe in yourself and dare to go your own way. When a reporter asked him how many sit-ups he could do, he replied: "I don't know. I start counting when it's starting to hurt. When I feel the pain, that's when I start counting. That's what counts!"

There really is a meaning to these wise words from a master. By doing what others cannot do today, you can tomorrow achieve what others cannot.

If you have followed the book, I hope you have opened your eyes to what life you can live and what wonderful opportunities that awaits you out there in the world, for those who dare to work for it. You are on your way to improving your health with your health goals and even your finances through your money goals. This chapter is about someone I hope you hold dear – yourself. To live a happy and successful life, it's important that you take care of yourself. You must decide what's important in your life. Your personal goals is about all the things that concern you. This can apply to your career or occupation, your interests – perhaps music or a particular sport – adventure and travel you dream about. Yes, it's only you who sets the limits. Your priorities in life probably depends on what stage you are in right now. If you have young children it's probably them you prioritize and it's difficult to have time for yourself. If you are young and single it might be all about you.

The important thing is that you take time for yourself – in whatever life situation you are in. By embracing your personal goals, you give yourself a chance to become a happier person.

THE STORY OF THE MEXICAN FISHERMAN

Before moving on to your career and your interests I want to tell you a story.

A very successful American stockbroker was on vacation with his family in a paradise-like fishing village somewhere on the Mexican Yucatán Peninsula. It was a small and quiet village where the beaches were unusually white, the sea was unusually green and crystal clear and the beer unusually cold and tasty. One night, the American stockbroker couldn't sleep, his mind had not had time to settle down from the hectic life on Wall Street in New York. He took a walk down to a bridge by the water where he sat down. The sea was calm and everything was so quiet that you could hear a pin drop to the ground.

A small boat docked and on the boat were several large and nice tuna fish.

The American praised the Mexican fisherman for his catch and asked how long it took to catch them. "Only a little while," replied the fisherman. "Why weren't you at sea longer to catch more fish?" asked the American.

The fisherman said that he had caught enough fish to support his family. The American stockbroker who came from a culture that constantly strove for more and more was confused.

"But what do you do with the rest of your time?"

"I sleep a few hours more, fish a little, play with my children and take a siesta with my wife," said the fisherman. "Every evening I stroll down to the village where I drink wine and play guitar with my amigos. I have a busy life."

The American said that he was a businessman and could

help the fisherman. "You should spend more time fishing and with the profits you can buy a bigger boat. With the proceeds from the bigger boat you could buy several boats and eventually you will have a whole bunch of boats. Instead of selling your catch to a middleman you can sell directly to the factory, until you eventually open your own cannery. Then you will control the product, production and distribution. Of course, you will have to move to Mexico City, LA and eventually to New York where you can manage the expanded operations."

"How long will it take?" asked the fisherman.

"15–20 years", replied the American.

"And then what?" asked the fisherman.

"That's the best part," laughed the American. "When the time is right, you'll do an IPO and sell shares in your company to the public. You will become very rich, you will make millions."

"Millions and then what?" asked the fisherman. "Then you could retire. You can move to a small fishing village where you can sleep a few hours more, fish a little, play with your children and take a siesta with your wife. In the evenings you can stroll down to the village, drink wine and play guitar with your amigos."

I think the story of the American stockbroker and the Mexican fisherman is very interesting. Take a moment to think about what this story means to you. What can you learn from the fisherman? So many people get caught up in the "rat race", they remain in the same routines that they do day in and day out without thinking about whether it's the way they really want their life to look like. The nice thing is that you are here today and reading this book – you want to create a life where you live the life you want. A first step is to think about your personal goals, so let's go.

⤳ ☆ ⤳

BY EMBRACING YOUR PERSONAL GOALS,

*you give yourself
a chance to become
a happier person.*

CAREER

"Do what you love and you'll never work another day in your life." / Confucius

Regardless of age, we have all at some point been children. We have also been asked: "What do you want to be when you grow up?" What did you want to be when you were little? Is it what you are today? Or have your dreams and goals changed? Maybe you've pushed aside the things you really want to do? If you're happy with what you do today, then congratulations, you have found the right place. For those of you who have not yet figured out what you want to do or have ended up on the wrong track – now is your chance to change that. There are different attitudes towards work and career. Some think that work is a necessary evil in order to pay their bills and others love their profession and find it difficult to break away from work. A study by the Wise Group shows that the job is the third most important factor to be happy, right behind health and a stable personal finance.

The job factors affecting the feeling of happiness most is development and to be proud of their employer. The happiness study also shows that those who have fun at work have better health and are happier in general.

Interestingly enough, it doesn't matter if you are a nurse, working in a factory or part of the management group of a large company, what's affecting happiness is the sense of pride, purpose and experiencing development. The conclusion we can draw from this study and many others who have shown similar results, is that what matters most is that you are doing something that you enjoy.

DARE TO TRY

Some know exactly what they want to work with, for others it's more difficult. It's therefore important that you dare to try new things. How will you otherwise know how it is? Many of us are living in a false bubble where we dream about something that we haven't actually tried or done anything about to achieve. For example, if you dream of becoming a lawyer, contact a law firm and ask for an internship there. Perhaps it's much more fun than you expected or it's much more tedious. But without actually trying things it's hard to know what really is fun and rewarding. And who knows, you might have a talent for something you've never tried.

I have learned to step outside my own comfort zone. This has involved that I have experienced many things and seen many places, but above all, I sit here today doing what I love – helping other people succeed. But the journey was very bumpy and I have tried several things that were not my thing. When I dropped out of college, my parents, friends and others around me thought I was stupid. What would become of me? But I knew deep down that I didn't want to sit in an office all day and count numbers. I wanted to create something of my own, I wanted to influence the world.

By going my own way – many times without the support from others – I have managed to move all the way from Sweden to Los Angeles, become one of the best salespeople in a company with over 500 employees, competing for the Swedish national team of karate for over ten years and win a lot of competitions in karate, including eight national championships and a bronze in the 2012 World Championship (Shotokan) in Sydney, Australia. I'm now heading towards my main goal in life: to help others to succeed and to live a wonderful life in LA.

Small, small steps every day can take you anywhere. Therefore, be sure to support yourself even when others don't. It's your life and you only have one, be sure to make something good out of it.

EXERCISE

What would you have done in life if money and time was not limited to you? How would your days look like? What would you work with? Where would you live? And so on.

- » Write down how your life would look like if you could do whatever you wanted. Don't set any limits, think big and have fun with this exercise.
- » What would have to happen in your life for you to achieve this? Who knows – maybe you could create the life you desire. I know you can. But do you believe in yourself?

NOTE: DO THE EXERCISE NOW! Good luck.

INTERESTS

Interest is a English noun meaning "something (especially an activity) that a person enjoys learning about or doing."

There are many different types of activities that can be really fun and give a lot in return. For me, my biggest interest, karate, has taken me around the world. It has meant that I met people I never would have met otherwise. It has made me feel that I'm part of something that I love and get to share it with other people who have the same interest.

Hopefully you have many interests. Life has so much to offer, so why not take advantage of it. Music, dance, art, books, sports, games, gardening, animals, cars, astrology, mathematics, yes, the list never ends. For those looking there is a lot you can do in your spare time. By having one or more interests, you can enhance the joy of living and for some, the interest will even become an occupation.

I don't know where in your life you are but one thing you should know, no matter how busy you are, how much you work, how many children you have or how many bills you have to pay, you need to take the time each week to do something just for yourself. If it's only an hour, you should ensure that it really is your hour and that you're doing something that you really are interested in. You may share some interests with your friends, your true love, your parents or your children so you can do the activity together, others you may want to do alone.

Never forget that life consists of time and it's you who decide how to spend it. It's intended that life should be fun and wonderful. Think about it: you live in the USA, one of the most amazing countries in the world. You are safe, you have a roof over your head, clothes on your body and food on the table. What more could you ask for?

With this kind of safety and support to back you up, you have the opportunity to create the life you desire. You deserve it! And don't forget that everything starts with some kind of interest, why did you for example begin to read this book? Sometimes it can be difficult to "see the forest for the trees" but I'm convinced that even if you find it difficult to find an interest you have at least a few things that you enjoy doing, but you might not perceive them purely as interests today. You may love coffee, cooking, play soccer or have a passion for flowers. Why not learn more about these topics, either on your own or through a membership in an association or club. There are associations or clubs for virtually everything. So if you want to meet people who share your interests, it's great to join an association or club.

It's up to you to take command of your life and do something good, something nice and enjoyable of it.

Did you know that the average American watches TV more than five hours per day and browses the internet more than one hour each day? If we add the use of mobile phones we're up to about seven, eight hours per day that the average American spends in front of a screen. TV, Internet and mo-

≪ ☆ ≫

NEVER FORGET THAT LIFE CONSISTS OF TIME

*and it's you who decide
how to spend it.
It's intended that life
should be fun and wonderful.*

bile phones are amazing inventions, but, when you're old and gray-haired, do you really want to look back on your life and realize that you have missed out on a whole lot of fun in the world just because you spent more than a quarter of your life in front of a screen? Think about it. Imagine that your life is like a cake, the most delicious cake you know. About a quarter of the cake you spend watching television and browsing the Internet, a second quarter you spend on sleeping and another quarter you spend working. The little that's left of the cake is the short time you have to do something sensible, interesting and fun. It's not that much, right?

Now imagine the same cake, but whole. Now, you decide exactly what you want to do with the pieces. How does it feel? Isn't it fun to be able to influence your life, create and do what you want? My best tip is that you stop logging in to Facebook 20 times a day and reduce your time watching TV. Life is here and now! Venture out and try new things, discover your interests and enjoy the short time you have here on earth.

EXERCISE

Decide to try one or a couple of new interests today. It may be something you have always wanted to do but never had the chance to. It can also be something you have stopped doing, but have the desire to take up again. If you cannot think of something interesting, do some research to find out what activities is offered nearby and find suitable activities you can try. Good luck!

TRAVEL AND ADVENTURE

Sun, sea and paradise beaches, cities and shopping, rock climbing in Nepal or wild animal safari in Africa? Or why not swim with pink dolphins in Peru, visit the pyramids in Egypt, celebrate New Year in Las Vegas or visit the Taj Mahal in India.

The world is an amazing place full of adventures and it should be explored. I love travelling and adventures and hope you do too. I have visited more than 20 countries on four continents and even though I'm only 27 years old, I have been travelling in total for more than three years. There is something special about travelling, the feeling of venturing out into new and unexplored lands: "What will I see? Who will I meet? What will I experience?

SOMETIMES YOU HAVE TO CLIMB DOWN FROM YOUR OWN MOUNTAIN

A great Japanese karate champion, who also was a very wise man once said:"Sometimes you have to climb down from your own mountain and onto another. Only then you can see how beautiful your own mountain is."

Just as the wise karate champion pointed out, it's important for those who can, to dare to discover the world. By embarking on new adventures, you get the opportunity to meet people that you would never had met and experience things that you never would have experienced. And sometimes you need to leave your own home and your own secure existence to actually understand how fortunate you are. And if it would happen that you find a place that suits you better, why not make a plan to move there or buy a small vacation home there? One of the best reasons to travel is precisely that it's an adventure, you don't really know what's going to happen. Some trips can be life-changing. I, for example, met the love of my life on a trip and I don't even want to think about how life would have been like if I hadn't made that trip.

EXERCISE

Let's have fun and play around a little. Write down a list of your ten dream destinations. This is what my list looks like:

» Go to Okinawa with my father.
» Celebrate New Year's in Las Vegas.
» Go to Rio de Janeiro during the carnival.
» Thailand.
» Los Angeles.
» Stay with monks in Tibet.
» Swim in the Devil's Pool in Victoria Falls, Zambia.
» Go on expedition to Antarctica.
» Hike up to Pelister's Eyes in Macedonia.
» Visit the Oktoberfest in Munich.

Dare to dream big. With the help of your willpower and this book, you can actually achieve exactly what you want. Imagine the adventures that awaits you. All dreams can turn into goals, which in turn can become reality.

PASSION

Before we finish this chapter and it's time for you to set your personal goals we are going to talk about passion.

All of us have probably met a person with a great passion for something particular and they sure are amazing!

You can have a passion for anything, for example for your family, money, travel, sports or anything else.

Just by talking to another person who has a great passion for something, you get filled up with energy and want to do something good for yourself. Passionate people have decided to pursue what they love and there is nothing that can stop them – and I really mean nothing. Problems become opportunities and setbacks turn into lessons. How can a person who refuses to fail not succeed? If you want to get inspired by someone with real passion, I recommend you to read the little book The Go-Getter, by Peter B. Kyne. The book is about Bill Veck, a war veteran from World War II who refuses to take no for an answer.

Some get envious of passionate people. "Who are you to be better than I am?" says the envious. "Who are you to not take hold of your life and make the best of it?" I would say. You're too smart to be that stupid to live your life the way other people want you to live, instead live life the way that makes you happy.

Remember that each one of us on this planet is unique. Everyone can succeed in what they want by turning their dreams into goals and their goals into reality. And you have now taken the step to take charge of your life, write down your goals and work towards them. Just by doing that you will get far, that I promise you.

FIND YOUR PASSION

Have you found your passion? If so, congratulations – keep going! If you haven't yet done so, here are some tips that can help you. Once you have made up your mind to find your passion, you make an important commitment to yourself. And the best part is that your whole attitude towards life becomes more positive, life becomes more fun and you become a better person.

WHAT ARE YOU GOOD AT?

Everyone is good at something. You don't need to be the best at what you do, the most important is that you enjoy it, that time passes quickly when you are doing the activity. An interest can be developed into a passion.

DARE TO TRY NEW THINGS

Most people's lives are quite similar from day to day. If you haven't yet found your passion, chances are that you won't just stumble upon it. In order to find something that arouses your passion, you must be open to new experiences. Dare to try new things even though they may not seem so fun at first sight. Who knows – you might like them. As for me, I never thought I would write a book about setting goals and how to succeed in life.

TALK TO THOSE WHO HAVE DONE WHAT YOU WANT TO DO.
If you still aren't sure if your interest can become something you really love, get ready to ask questions. Get in touch with people and talk to those who are already doing what you want to do. Ask any questions you want answered. You will be amazed at how helpful people who are passionate about something are.

PRACTICE AND EXPLORE
Some know immediately what their passion is, others may work at it for a long time. Remember that you don't need to find your passion overnight. Run through and practice your interests. Examine the topics you are interested in by reading books and look it up online.

FACE YOUR FEARS
One way to find your passion in life can be by facing your fears. Fear is often seen as a negative feeling, but it's a strong feeling just like passion. Sometimes you might be afraid of something because you really care about it. Maybe you're afraid to fail with something that you've always wanted to be good at. Work to explore and manage your fears – they can at best lead you to your passion.

NEVER GIVE UP
Once you have found your passion, decide to never give up. To succeed in something takes struggle and many hours of hard work. Get through adversities and enjoy the successes. Believe in yourself! Even if you haven't found your passion in life, keep the spirit up my friend and get help from the tips above, I'm convinced that you will succeed. And to those who have found it: be happy and live passionately.

THE 10,000-HOUR RULE

For those who want to become experts in a field it's important to know the 10,000-hour rule. Many times we look at successful people with envy and think: "If only I had such a talent, if only I was born there, if only I had been as lucky as her." The excuses are many for those who are afraid to work for their success. Behind almost every successful person there is a unique story that often involves a lot of hardships and very hard work for several years. Look at some of the best soccer players in the world, such as Zlatan Ibrahimovic, a real soccer king. Doesn't it look easy when he's dribbling past player after player? It seems easy to be Zlatan. Drive a Ferrari, play some ball and eat baguettes in Paris. If we scratch the surface a little (if you get the chance: read his book!) and actually get to know Zlatan, we realize that he's a man with character, a man who never lets himself be discouraged, although he was always misunderstood and discouraged when he was young.

Zlatan and many other successful people are successful precisely because they never gave up, they continued passionately forward no matter what happened. That's the reason they have succeeded.

Many writers, scientists, trainers and coaches have tried to find out what it takes to really be successful in one particular field. Interestingly enough, everyone seem to come to the same conclusion: it takes 10,000 hours of work to become an expert at what you do. This means that if you spend three hours a day on a task it takes ten years to become an expert. Unfortunately, we live in a world today where everything must happen fast, we want everything now and if we cannot get it, we give up.

With the knowledge that it takes many years to get good at something, you don't need to be so hard on yourself if it's not going that well in the beginning. Don't give up, continue forward and learn from your mistakes. If you keep it up long enough, you will eventually become an expert. Did you know that the competition is not as tough at the top? It's easier to achieve something great than something small. It's because most people don't believe in themselves or are not ready to put in the work that is required. So dare to aim big in life and don't be surprised if you actually succeed. And time will pass anyway, it cannot be stopped, so why not make something good of it?

TASK: PERSONAL GOALS

Now it's time to set your personal goals. They will take you closer to the life you want to live and above all, they will help you become the person you want to be. But first I want you to answer the following questions. Be honest with yourself.

a. What are you most satisfied with in your life right now?
b. What are you least satisfied with in your life right now?
c. Does your days look the way you wish? If not, what would you like to change?

Use these answers when you are setting your personal goals. Take the chance to change what you want to change. It's your life, you deserve to have a career you enjoy, you deserve to have interests that you love, you deserve to see the world and you deserve to be passionate.

» Write down at least one and maximum three personal goals, which are goals that are related to your career or your interests. Or why not turn your interest into your career? Dare to set a high goal, remember the 10,000-hour rule.
» Write down in a few lines what it will mean for your life when you achieve your goals.
» Set a deadline.
» Make an activity plan.
» Set sub-goals.
» Do something today that will take you towards your goal.

Here you will get two examples of personal goals that are taken from my own life. If you've followed the book so far, you have already taken a few steps forward when it comes to your health and financial goals. If you've done your homework, you start to understand that it really is not that hard to get ahead in life, the important thing is to decide what you want to do, write it down, set a deadline and plan how to get there. The more you work with goals, the greater successes you will reap. But remember that whatever you achieve in your life, a balance between all areas of life is the most important thing to be happy.

EXAMPLE 1. CAREER

Goal: Start my own business that becomes successful.

When I become a successful entrepreneur it will make me very happy. Every day, I work for myself and for a better world. By delivering my products and services, my clients will increase their vitality and become happier, which in turn will give me great satisfaction. By being my own boss, I will be able to influence my income and my work hours, which will lead to a life on my own terms.

Deadline: Three years

Activity plan:
  - » Create a business plan.
  - » Develop products and services.
  - » Market the business.
  - » Actively seek clients.
  - » Do a good job.
  - » Through daily hard work and good reputation, grow into a successful business.

Sub-goal 1: Create a business plan within a month.

Reward: Dinner at my favorite restaurant with my girlfriend.

Sub-goal 2: Register the company within three months.
Reward: The satisfaction of being one step closer to the dream.

Sub-goal 3: Have at least five paying customers within six months.
Reward: Buy an iPad mini.

Sub-goal 4: Have a minimum of 20 paying customers within a year.
Reward: Celebrate with family and friends.

Ultimate Goal: A successful and profitable business within three years.
Reward: Dream trip to Thailand.

To do today to get me closer to my goal: Write at least two pages of the business plan.

EXAMPLE 2. HOBBIES

This goal is taken from my real life and is written down just as in my private notes. The goal was set on August 1, 2012. A little more than three months later, I stood at the Sydney Olympic Sports Centre in Australia with a bronze medal from the World Championships in Shotokan karate around my neck. It was my life's greatest achievement. Would I had come third in the World Championships without writing down my goals and make a plan to achieve them? I don't think so.

Goal: My goal is that I will at the World Championships in Sydney, November 19–24, 2012, be in the best shape of my life physically and mentally and that I will be able to bring out the best in me when it counts. If I manage to bring out the best I got, I know that I'm a winner and a medal candidate at the World Championships.

How? I will succeed by doing the following actions:

- » Good exercise plan.
- » Develop my mental ability.
- » Develop my physical ability.
- » Bring out the best of my karate.
- » Take advantage of my experience.
- » Focus on my own performance.
- » Good diet.
- » Have fun.
- » Bring out the true champion and warrior within me.
- » Believe in myself – no one can budge me.
- » I am a winner.

When? On November 19–24, 2012.

In addition to this, I wrote, in consultation with my coach (and father), down an exercise plan week by week. Also, I had a few competitions before the World Championships as sub-goals to test my performance. I also printed out a sheet of paper, which I clearly could see in my apartment several times every day, with the text:

Goal: Being in the best shape of my life and show it!

There you go, now it's your turn. Write down your goals now, don't wait. Aim high and go for it, you will be rewarded.

☙ ✩ ☙

RELATIONSHIP GOALS

"Where there is love there is life."

/ Mahatma Gandhi

Nice work, if you've come this far in the book, it means that you are a determined and disciplined person on your way towards the life you want to live. You are a person with a mission that refuses to be discouraged. If that happens, you rise up and continue forward. You are an amazing and unique person and I'm proud to make this journey with you.

We have come a long way and gone through your health, your financial and your personal goals. Now it's time to talk about relationships. Your relationships with your partner, your family, your friends and yourself. What would for example, great financial success mean if you don't have friends, family or even a good relationship with yourself? Unfortunately it's all too common in today's modern society that we focus everything on becoming successful and somewhere along the way we lose ourselves and those around us. But with the help of your strong will and the tools from this book, you can create a balanced, successful and happy life in all areas.

A man who really understands what has happened too many of us in today's world is the wise Tibetan Buddhist and monk Dalai Lama. This is what he says in the text of *The Paradox of Our Times*:

* We have bigger houses, but smaller families.
* More conveniences, but less time.

* We have more degrees, but less sense.
* More knowledge, but less judgment.
* More experts, but more problems.
* More medicines, but less wellness.
* We've been all the way to the moon and back, but have trouble crossing the street to meet the new neighbor.
* We build more computers to hold more information, to produce more copies than ever, but we have less communication.
* We've become long on quantity but short on quality.
* We have fast food, but slow digestion.
* These are the times of tall men, and short character.
* Steep profits and shallow relationships.
* We have a lot of windows, but it's empty in the rooms.

I think Dalai Lama explains it very well. It's easy to be blinded by everything that "glitters" and forget many of the truly important values in life such as love, respect, humility, kindness, generosity and more. But through knowledge and understanding you have the opportunity to think differently and actually take the time to become a better person – this will make both you and all your fellow human beings happier.

LOVE

What is love? This fantastic and wonderful feeling that is almost impossible to describe. If you have experienced love at some time you know exactly how it feels. If you haven't experienced love yet, don't give up, it's worth all the waiting in the world. Love is something you feel for another person or being, it can be your boyfriend or girlfriend, one of your siblings, parents, or maybe a pet. Butterflies in the stomach, nervousness, sweating and joy can all be a part of being in love – everyone experiences love differently, but it's still the same thing. If love is reciprocated, it feels wonderful, but if it's unanswered, it can feel like your whole world is falling apart. One thing is quite certain: if you give a lot of love to your surroundings, you will receive a lot of love back in one way or another.

Just like we talked about earlier, it's very important to feel appreciated and loved to live a successful and happy life. Therefore, you must make time for your relationships and for love. Never forget that even if you have a very successful career, are young and strong and have a lot of money, it can never replace love. True love is the people around you who are happy when you succeed, but that also lifts you up and supports you when everything falls to pieces.

In this chapter you will learn more about how you can make your relationships with your fellow human beings better. You will also learn how to attract the people you want in your life and how you say no to the people who hurt you in some way or another. But the very first tip you'll get from me when it comes to love and relationships is to trust your gut. If it feels right, it is usually right. Also remember that the more love you give, the more you get in return.

EXERCISE

Starting today and ten days forward, at the same time each day, you will devote at least ten minutes writing down what you are grateful for and feel love for in your life. Write freely and let it come from your heart. The first time you do this it might feel difficult, but persevere and continue to think. I'm convinced that there are hundreds of things you can be grateful for and feel love for.

- » Write down freely what you are grateful for and/or feel love for in your life.
- » Write for at least ten minutes.
- » Write at the same time each day for ten days.

This exercise will help you see how much love and gratitude you actually already have in your life.

FAMILY

What is your family like? All families are different, and no one is perfect. I can say that after having visited the home of many families. There are many preconceptions about how a family should be constructed. In today's society, families, however, can all look differently and that's okay. The most important thing is that there is love in the home. By feeling safe and loved at home you build a joy and faith in life that makes everything so much easier. And is there anything more beautiful than having a good relationship with your mother, father and siblings?

Hopefully you have been born into a family full of love and tenderness, where you have been able to learn what it takes in life to be able to stand on your own two feet. But you cannot choose your parents and if you have or have had problems with your family, it's important to understand that there are solutions to everything. You are not alone, many people have managed to overcome the obstacles at home and moved on in life to create the future they desire.

THE STORY OF THE TWINS

There is a story of two twin brothers whose father was an alcoholic. Growing up with abuse in the family was very difficult for these twins. Every day was full of problems. Some days the father was very happy and everything was hunky-dory but other days he was blind drunk, screaming and throwing things around. The mother always tried to do her best to support their children, even if it was very tough. To be able to support the household, she had to take two jobs, but the money was still never really enough. When the brothers got older they sometimes wanted to go to the movies with their friends or to have a new pair of pants, but it was difficult for the mother to give that to her children. Years went by and it was tough for the children both at home and at school. They never really felt any security within themselves.

⤸ ☆ ⤸

TRUST YOUR GUT FEELING.

If it feels right,
it is usually right.
Also remember that
the more love you give,
the more you get in return.

15 years later the twins were approached by a newspaper that wanted to do a story about them. It turned out that one of the twins had defied all odds. He had, through hard work managed to become one of the country's top lawyers. For the other brother, things had not turned out that well. His life had been marked by problems both with the law and with himself and he was now an alcoholic.

The reporter asked the two brothers separately why they had ended up just where they were. Interestingly enough, he got the same answer: "I had no choice, my dad was an alcoholic."

Moral of the story: you choose how you want to handle what happens in life – either you see it as an opportunity or you see yourself as a victim. One of the twins chose to turn the big family problem into a motivation to succeed while the other brother saw himself as a victim and therefore had no choice but to end up just like his dad.

In the same way as these brothers, you choose how your life will look like. You cannot control who your mom, dad and your siblings are. But if you have or have had it tough at home for any reason, you can choose whether it should be a spark to a better life or whether you should play the victim role. And the day you form your own family, make sure to do everything it takes to make it as good as possible for all of you.

Remember that without love and happiness, it doesn't matter how successful you are in other areas of life. The road to feel fully satisfied and successful is through love and happiness.

FIND YOUR LIFE PARTNER

Have you ever wondered what the meaning of life is? You are not alone, most people have probably asked themselves that question. I don't have the answer but one of the greatest desires in life for many is to find a life partner and form their own family. Have you found someone to share your life with – congratulations! – continue to work on your relationship every day and never take your partner for granted. If you haven't yet found your life partner, continue to live your life and do what you love, then you will attract the right kind of people in your life. And for those who are not looking for someone to share your life with: be sure to take good care of yourself and learn to love yourself.

Did you know that almost half of all marriages in the USA end in divorce? When you hear these gloomy figures, one wonders if it's really worth investing in love. Must it be so difficult? One of the biggest reasons that we don't manage our relationships is that we feel pressure from different directions and that time is short. It costs to be on top and the dream of owning a beautiful house, having two cars and enough time for your family is not always easy to fulfill. Unfortunately, many start-up families begin at the wrong end with big loans and credits. A new house, two cars and a lot of installments. To be able to have the lifestyle and keep your head above water, many work very hard and the little time you're free, you're often tired and irritated. Conflicts are created and if you already feel bad, you might not be very responsive and smooth when trying to solve them. This way many good relationships get destroyed. Couples who once loved each other become strangers.

It doesn't have to be this way. You can choose to be different. You can choose to live a life with a nice and happy family where you never take anything for granted.

EXERCISE

Here is an exercise that helps you find your life partner.

TO GET WHAT YOU WANT, YOU MUST KNOW WHAT YOU WANT.
Imagine a sailboat who embarks on a journey without destination. If the crew are lucky maybe it will come to a beautiful

beach somewhere in the world, if they are unlucky, they will end up in the middle of a storm and capsize. It can be the same thing in a relationship.

Some are very strongminded about how their prospective partner should look like or what background they should have. For others it's important that you share the same interests and values. It's up to you how you want your partner to be, but the worst thing you can do is to settle for anyone that comes your way. Don't let chance decide your future life partner. If you are lucky, he or she might become like a beautiful beach somewhere in the world but if you are unlucky, you might end up in the middle of a storm.

Take the chance to form the family you desire and have the courage to go after the life partner that fits you!

» Write down how you would like your dream partner to be. Write down everything you wish her or him to be like and how your life together will look like.

» Write down who you need to be and what your life needs to look like for you to be able to attract this person.

If you already found your dream partner, write down what you can do to maintain the glow and happiness in your life.

Don't make the mistake that many people make. They invest everything in education, career or a hobby, but let chance decide who they share the rest of their life with. You deserve to have someone who enhances the quality of your life. You deserve someone who laughs with you and rejoice in your success. You deserve someone who lifts you up when everything falls to pieces and stands by your side if the rest of the world is against you. But never forget: before you can attract that person in your life you must act. By offering another human being all of this, you will in turn have the opportunity to receive the same from somebody else.

FRIENDS

How we value friendships can be very different, some of us would take a bullet for our friend while others may see a friend more as entertainment when you are bored. No matter how you perceive the friendship it's important to have friends. Alone we are strong, but together we are stronger. By having good relationships with your family, partner and friends, your joy in life increases. Additionally, you can with your knowledge help your friends while they can help you with their knowledge.

Nowadays, we have hundreds of friends on Facebook but no one to call in a crisis. I know many people but there are few I can call friends. There are not very many that I could call if I was on the other side of the globe and needed someone to come and help me. Imagine yourself in this situation: you are far from home and something serious has happened. Do you have any friends you could call that would hop on the first flight to help you? If we are to be completely honest with each other, it's probably few that have such a friend, sadly enough. But it's not that strange if we turn the question around – "How many friends do you have that you would help by taking the first flight to the other side of the globe?" – what would the answer be then?

For me, friendship always begins with myself. In order to have good friends, I must be a good friend myself. We often speak of unconditional love or friendships but such a relationship is from the beginning always based on an exchange. If you wish to have some real friends in life you can have fun with and who stands up for you, you must begin with yourself. Do you stand up for your friends or do you always think of yourself?

Spring is coming and this weekend my girlfriend and I and some of my closest friends went out for a few beers. After a discussion, I told one of my friends: "I know you will succeed.

Within five years, you are the coach of a big soccer team."

On the way home, my girlfriend was wondering how I could know that. The answer is that I don't know, I can never know. But he is my friend and I believe in him, so why should I not tell him that? By giving him the compliment I might make him fight a little harder. He hopefully thinks: "Peter believes in me, even though it will be difficult I think I can succeed."

Dare to give a little of yourself to your friends, dare to believe in them. You will notice that it feels good to give and receive happiness to other people. And you know what, you will get much more in return. Because it's much more fun to give to someone that you have received something from.

YOUR SURROUNDINGS SHAPES YOU

In order to succeed in your life one important thing is required of you: that you are honest with yourself and look around at your surroundings. If you want to reach your goals you need to have good and positive people around you. First and foremost, you must believe in yourself and in the end listen to your own words, but it's also important to be surrounded by the right kind of personalities. Do you have a friend or relative who sees everything from a negative angle? I'm a person with many ideas and during a time in my life I had some friends who were very negative. Every idea I came up with was perceived as "bad" or "impossible" to succeed with. Fortunately, I have now decided not to meet with them as often and additionally, I would never share my ideas with them – if not to annoy them a little.

If you want to live a happy and successful life, look over your immediate circle. Do you have any people around you that are just taking instead of giving energy? People who are negative towards whatever you might share with them? Make sure to spend time with these people as seldom as possible. You should be surrounded by people who lift you up, who

ᘒ ☆ ᘒ

YOU CHOOSE HOW YOU WANT TO HANDLE

what happens in life.
Either you see it as
an opportunity or you
see yourself as a victim.

want to help you and want to see you succeed. Naturally, there will always be people who are negative, especially the more successful you will be. The important thing is to make sure to remove them from your life as much as possible. By sharing your day with positive and creative people you will become a better person yourself. Or, as my father so nicely put it: "Life is what you make of it, don't waste energy on unnecessary things in life."

LIFE

We are born, we live and we die. Imagine that your life is like a book, the world's best book and it's you who must decide what it will contain. You can fill each page with anything you want. When you are born, the pages are completely blank, it's you who must decide what should be on them. How would you have written your book?

Many of us live as if our book has an endless amount of pages "it doesn't matter if I skip a few pages." But don't you want your book (life) to be as good as possible? Just as it's important to pursue good relations with the family, partner and friends, it's important that you seek a good relationship to life itself. You have only one life and believe it or not, it goes fast. Therefore, ensure that you create a positive and good attitude to life. I have said it before and I'll say it again: it's your life and you choose how it will look like. The majority of the days you live, you should feel joy for. When you wake up and look at yourself in the mirror, you should feel like you are on the right path. Do you wake up too many days in a row with a bad feeling and are not happy with the person you see in the mirror then it's time for a change. With the tools from this book, you can change your approach to life. Remember that it's you who decide. Life passes by quickly so make sure to take charge of it now!

YOURSELF

Soon it's time for you to develop your relationships and set your first relationship goal. But before we go any further, let's talk about the most important relationship you have in life, the one with yourself. There is no one who can help you more than you, on the other hand, there is no one that can destroy more for yourself than just you. Everyone has an inner dialogue with themselves and many times, we ourselves are the biggest reason why we fail.

Play with the idea that you are behind a scene. You will soon go in and speak to ten thousand people. What do you say to yourself just before you go on stage?

Do you say: "Come on, I can handle this, I'm the best and know just what to say. Besides, what's the difference from speaking before hundreds of people as I have done many times before? I can handle this."

Or do you say: "Damn, shit, I can't do this. How will I be able to speak in front of so many people? I don't want to. I cannot talk in front of others. I suck, what have I gotten myself into?"

Which inner dialogue will make you perform your best do you think? Obviously, it's the first dialogue that makes the chances for success increase significantly. By talking to yourself in a positive way, you will become happier, perform better and be more successful. Hopefully you have begun working with the exercises in Chapter Four and already improved your inner dialogue.

Everything in this book really begins and ends with the relationship to yourself and it's therefore important that you develop a good self-confidence and a good self-esteem. If you've done the exercises so far in the book and started with your new goals in life, I'm sure that your belief in yourself has grown and that you're starting to feel a greater joy in life.

However, all change is difficult in the beginning and it comes down to doing your homework every day, even when it feels tough. Suddenly your routines and your whole life has changed for the better.

TASK: RELATIONSHIP GOALS

Good work. You've come a long way and you're starting to become awesome at setting goals. Hopefully, you have by now understood that you can succeed with almost anything if you have the courage to strive for what you want. And you know what, even if you wouldn't reach all the way, you will come a lot further than if you had never tried.

IT'S NOW TIME FOR YOU TO SET YOUR FIRST RELATIONSHIP GOALS

1. Get a pen and paper, because now it's time. Your first task is to write down everything you would like to improve with your relationships. It can be anything (see example) and as much as you would like. Dare to write down exactly what you would like to achieve: which friends you want in your life, what kind of relationship you want with your partner, the relationship you want to yourself etc. Set no limits and for now don't think of what you will have to do to achieve this.

EXAMPLE

» I want to improve my relationship with my sister.
» I want to avoid negative people in my life.
» I want to attract new positive people in my life.
» I want to improve my confidence and my self-esteem.
» I want to be a better boyfriend.

2. Read through what you have written and choose at least one and maximum three goals to work towards.
» I want to improve my relationship with my sister.
» I want to avoid negative people in my life.
» I want to improve my confidence and my self-esteem.

3. You have now picked out a few things that you feel are important for improving your relationships right now. Write down in a few sentences what it would mean for you when you succeed in achieving these goals.

EXAMPLE

IMPROVE THE RELATIONSHIP WITH MY SISTER

By achieving this goal, my quality of life will increase. If I cannot have a good relationship with my sister or my family and friends no other successes matter. These relationships will create joy, laughter, adventure and memories for life.

AVOID NEGATIVE PEOPLE

By avoiding negative people in my life, I will succeed better in my life. Instead of spending unnecessary energy on negative people, I will be able to devote my time to positive people who bring joy into my life.

IMPROVE MY CONFIDENCE AND MY SELF-ESTEEM

By improving my confidence and my self-esteem my life will be better. By having the strength to believe in myself even when everything doesn't go as it should, I will dare to continue toward my goals. This will increase my chances for a better life and the chance for me to achieve my goals.

Now you have come up with a few things that you'd like to improve with your relationships. You have also written down what it would mean for you to achieve these goals. Before you make a plan to achieve your goals, it's time to set a time limit. Remember that a goal without a deadline is not a goal. Carefully consider how long it can take to achieve your goals. It's important that you set a time limit that makes your goal motivating, meaning that the goal may not be so short that you feel you are not capable of accomplishing it. On the other hand, it can't be so far away that you forget your goal.

When it comes to your relationships, it can sometimes be difficult to calculate how long it takes to achieve your goals because relationships are something you work on constantly. If you have trouble setting a deadline regarding your relationship goals you can instead set a deadline on the activities you do to achieve your ultimate goal. With these activity goals you can easily influence and measure yourself.

In my case, I want to improve my relationship with my sister. I can't know how she will react to what I do, but I can still make a plan of activities that I think would improve our relationship. For these activities I can set a deadline.

EXAMPLE

Goal 1: Improve my relationship with my sister.
Time limit: Six months.

Goal 2: Avoid negative people in my life.
Time limit: Two months.

Goal 3: Improve my confidence and my self-esteem.
Time limit: Six months.

You have now written down your goals, what it will mean for you when you achieve them and when to achieve them. Now comes the most important thing, to make a plan for how you will achieve them. Your plan will include sub-goals and activities required to achieve your goals.

EXAMPLE

IMPROVE MY CONFIDENCE AND MY SELF-ESTEEM

Time limit: Six months
Activity Plan:
* Start a mental training program.
* Read books about self-confidence and self-esteem.
* Make the necessary changes.

Sub-goal 1: After two months, I have conducted a mental training program.
Reward: The joy of having made progress.

Sub-goal 2: After four months, I have completed another mental training program and have read at least two books on self-confidence and self-esteem.
Reward: A day off from work to do what I want.

Ultimate Goal: After six months, I have carried out a third mental training program and read at least two more books about self-confidence and self-esteem. I'll also have made the changes necessary to increase my confidence and my self-esteem.
Reward: A weekend in Las Vegas with my girlfriend.

Good job. You are now on your way to better relationships, a very important part of a successful and happy life.

SOCIAL GOALS

"We make a living by what we get. We make a life by what we give."

/ Winston Churchill

It's getting time to wrap up your goals. Together we have come a long way towards the life you want to live. You have begun to think and look into how you live your life today and started to adjust your life in the direction you desire. Now it's time to deal with the final part: your social goals.

Just as relationship goals, the social goals can sometimes feel somewhat tougher, since it can be difficult to measure them. But it's equally important that you take hold of these parts of your life. These softer values are those that will actually give you the greatest joy. By developing your relationships and your social life you will be able to create a life where you are sincerely happy and have the ability to communicate with and attract the people you want in your life.

Do you remember the study of the Olympic medalists earlier in the book? It showed that the bronze medalists were happier than the silver medalists at the Olympics. The reason was that the bronze medalists felt that they won the bronze but the silver medalists felt that they lost the gold. This shows that true success and happiness is in your head. Although it sounds like a cliché, it's not what happens to you that is important but how you handle it.

It's the same thing in your social life. Have you ever woken up and felt really happy? A day where nothing can shake you is waiting. The sun is shining, the birds are singing and life is wonderful. Until you get to work and your manager (who has woken up on the wrong side) yells at you for a small mistake you made. You call a customer (who has also woken up on the wrong side) and get another scolding. What happens then?

If you're very strong mentally, you can hopefully shake this off and still maintain your good mood. If you haven't been training your mental ability, it can throw you completely off balance.

The manager and the customer are external factors that cannot always be influenced. But why would you let them affect your well-being? It's in such moments good social skills will come in handy. Maybe you can turn the manager's and the customer's bad mood with a joke or by calmly answering their questions. Our social skills are very different from person to person but no matter what level you are at today, it's important to work on it.

Because it's with your social skills that you will ultimately achieve what you want. You can be the hottest person in the world, but if you have trouble talking with someone you're attracted to, it becomes difficult to be able to catch her or him. You might be very well educated but lack social skills altogether. That means that your chances of landing that high-paying job decreases a lot. Deep down, I believe that everyone has something good within themselves and that we are all good at something. Some find it easily and others will have to try to see what works. Unfortunately, many fail to live the life they want because they don't take the time to develop their social skills.

THE FEAR OF BEING REJECTED

One of our most common and biggest fears is the fear of being rejected. The idea of being turned down by another person is scary. That's the reason why many are involuntarily singles, they don't dare to approach other people. They prefer to wait for someone else to approach them. And just as we discussed in the previous chapter that is why so many people end up with a partner they don't really want. They were afraid to approach other people and when they were approached they became excited. So excited that they forgot to actually see if the person in question shared the same values. Many people learn their lesson the hard way, with divorce and children who live every other week with their parents. Don't misunderstand me, even if you have good social skills and dare to approach people, you can of course attract the wrong kind of people in your life, but the chances of better relationships increases when you choose the people you want around you.

Have you ever been afraid to approach someone you felt attracted to? Have you been thinking something like: "What should I say? What if he/she is rude? Everyone is looking at me, what if I get rejected?" Most of us have probably at some point felt like this. Just the thought of being rejected scares most people and that is precisely why we must dare. What is the worst thing that can happen? Well, the worst thing that can happen is that you get a no, and what does that really matter? What if it turns out that this person actually is interested in you? It could be your future life partner or best friend. All relationships have begun as two strangers who somehow started to communicate. And if you would get a no, don't see it as a defeat, but rather see it as a confirmation that this is a person that you don't need in your life. Isn't it better to know than to live with the thought "what if"?

If you have worked as a salesperson like me, you have been privileged to learn how to handle rejection. Bad days as a salesman, you can get a no 50-100 times. I'd be lying if I said it's easy to get so many no's, but at the same time, I've learned to not take it personally. And as people in sales use to say: "Every

formatting: ℮ℓ ☆ ℓℯ

DID YOU KNOW THAT THE MOST IMPORTANT THING WHEN

you want to communicate
something to another person
is your body language
and tone of voice,
only a small proportion
are the words you actually say.

no is one step closer to a yes!" The best thing is that the more customers you call the better you become at communicating and the more yes you'll receive. The same applies to your social life. The more you talk to people you don't know, the better you become at communicating. It works exactly the same way as the fact that you have to exercise to improve your fitness level and that you need to save money in order to get more money.

EXERCISE

You will now start practicing your social skills. During the next ten days, approach at least two people every day that you have never talked to before. It can be on the bus, at work, in the elevator, at the café, yes anywhere you want. The important thing is that you start talking to new people.

If you feel uncomfortable, start with saying hello to a stranger or why not talk about the weather, the big news that just happened or something else. In just ten days, you will notice that it's not as scary as you might think. If you already believe that you are socially skilled, do the exercise anyway, who knows – you might get a date or a new acquaintance.

BODY LANGUAGE

Did you know that the most important thing when you want to communicate something to another person is your body language and tone of voice, only a small proportion are the words you actually say. Results vary a little between different studies but Albert Mehrabian, a Californian researcher who is often the one mentioned in this context, believes that 55 percent of communication comes from body language, 38 percent from the voice and only seven percent from the words. We don't need to care much about the numbers, but we can conclude that if you want to develop your social skills you need to work on your body language.

By developing your body language, you can increase your chances of being perceived in the way you wish.

Since I have been a top athlete in karate, I can attest to how much body language actually affect the surroundings. Every time I show up at a competition arena, I'm reminded of it. Everything begins in the locker room when my gaze meets the opponent's. I can immediately tell if my opponent is afraid of me because he looks away, or if he is there to fight and isn't afraid to meet my gaze. When warming up before the competition, you can often tell which people are medal candidates. Many of the best athletes radiate a strength of comfort and confidence when they walk around in there. They have a commanding presence and a calmness that those who are new hasn't yet had time to develop. You can see that they really want this and that they will do their absolute best to win. Before the competition starts, I can often feel if I'm going to win. When I stand face to face against my opponent, I feel if he's afraid of me. If I meet an opponent with a strong body expression as myself, I know it will be a very tight match. The one who remains focused during the entire competition will be successful. During the match, the opponents' body language or gaze can sometimes change, if I'm in the lead and the opponent is tired. Then I know that the match is mine.

As you see, we aren't talking with each other, yet we communicate. Similarly, you also convey a message to the people around you, whether you talk or not. Let's say you step into a room full of people standing tall and smiling. The minute after another person enters, the back is bent and the head is tilted downwards, gazing into the ground and the facial expression is sad. How do you think the people in the room look at the two of you? Well, you will certainly be perceived as a cheerful person with good self-esteem and the other person will be perceived as a sad person with low self-esteem and be less attractive in the eyes of the surroundings.

Here are seven tips to help you get a confident body language.

1. STAND UP STRAIGHT

A good posture radiates confidence. It's also healthy for your body.

2. LOOK AHEAD AND MAKE EYE CONTACT

A person looking down seems uncertain. Instead, look up and dare to meet other people's eyes. When you talk to others, look them in the eye, but don't stare. Now and then you look away to make the conversation comfortable. Also, avoid looking down when you walk alone. Look ahead and straighten up your posture, it radiates self-confidence.

3. STABLE HANDSHAKE

There is nothing worse when meeting new people than a weak or limp handshake. Shake hands with confidence with a stable hold of the person's hand. But remember, a handshake is not a competition. Do not crush the person's hand and don't hold it for too long.

4. AVOID CROSSED ARMS OR HANDS IN YOUR POCKETS

Avoid crossing your arms, it shows that you are nervous or on your guard. Don't have your hands in the pockets since you can be perceived as uncomfortable and unsure of yourself. Dare to have an open position where the hands rest freely, it signals confidence and shows that you have nothing to hide.

5. USE YOUR VOICE

Speak slowly and clearly, it shows that you are relaxed and confident in yourself. Many tend to slur and speak faster when they are nervous or insecure. Studies show that those who varies their tone become more interesting to listen to. You can also create a better personal chemistry by adapting your volume and pace to the person you're talking to.

6. SMILE

Self-confident people smile because they have nothing to worry about. Try to smile at other people. You will be surprised how many people actually smile back.

7. DON'T SEEK APPROVAL

Don't seek approval from others when you talk to them. If you are constantly waiting for approval of what you said by wanting the person you're talking to agree with you, you can be perceived as insecure. Say what you want to say and have confidence in it! Everyone is entitled to their own opinion and it's important that you stand up for what you say.

By following these seven tips, you can develop your body language so that you communicate happiness, confidence and calmness. The best thing with a good body language is that it affects your mood. For example, try to smile as much as you can for five minutes while you at the same time try to be sad. It's almost impossible because the body language not only affects what you radiate to other people, it also affects your inner dialogue.

HOW DO YOU WANT TO COMMUNICATE?

How do other people see you? Do they perceive you in the way you want? It's just as important that you perceive yourself as you would like and that you convey the same feeling to your surroundings.

I don't know how good your social skills are today, but we can all improve our communication with other people. Sometimes you can feel misunderstood or inferior in a certain group, but by learning to convey the message you wish, chances of a clear and good communication increases.

I'm convinced that the world would have been much better

if more people had good social skills. Imagine if we could sit down and solve the problems that arise in peace. Many wars would end, more joy would be created and many relationships would be saved.

Whether you already have good social skills, or feel that you lack communication skills with other people, it's important that you want to develop and that you want to learn. You are on the right track in life, you are on your way to achieving your health goals, financial goals, personal goals and relationship goals. The only thing missing is that last little piece of the puzzle for everything to fall into place. By developing good social skills, you, as I have mentioned earlier, will get many advantages on life's journey.

An important factor when it comes to developing good social skills is that you make connections. By doing this, you also make friends. Friends who you can help and friends who can help you. Did you know that 75 percent of all jobs are filled through internal recruitment and personal contacts? Thus, three out of four jobs go to someone who the recruiter already had previous contact with. To make connections or networking, is very common in the business world. Many entrepreneurs have understood that it's important to help each other to succeed to get further. In the same way you can, by connecting with other people, build a wider circle of acquaintances and a larger network that will help you moving forward.

EXERCISE

Take out a pen and paper and write down some key words on how you want to be perceived by other people.

EXAMPLE

> » Calm
> » Confident
> » Happy

» Trustworthy
» Inspirational
» Interesting

TWO EARS AND ONE MOUTH

Many people have misunderstood how social skills work. You've probably met them, they just talk and talk and jump wildly between different subjects and stories that are not coherent at all. You try in vain to jump in or change the topic. These kinds of people have a monologue rather than a dialogue.

If you want to develop your social skills, it's a good idea to take into account what nature has given us: two ears and one mouth. A good rule of thumb when you are talking with others is to listen twice as much as you talk. Most people love to talk about themselves, provided that they feel comfortable in the situation and that the other person is actually listening and contributes to making it a good and friendly dialogue. A tip to have better conversations and become a better listener is to ask open questions.

Let's play with the idea that you're on a date and you're sitting down to eat a good meal. Because it's the first time you're out together, you should get to know each other. To get the conversation going, ask as few questions as possible where the answer can only be yes, no or I don't know. Rather ask questions which your date has to think about and give you a more detailed answer.

EXAMPLE

Yes/No question: Do you like travelling?
Open question: Tell me about your dream destination?

As you can see the conversation ends very quickly with a yes/no question while an open question invites to a nice dialogue. Remember to look the person in the eye when he or she talks

ꜵ ☆ ꜵ

IF YOU WANT TO DEVELOP YOUR SOCIAL SKILLS,

*it's a good idea
to take into account
what nature has given us:
two ears and one mouth.*

to you, but look away occasionally so that it's not perceived as you're staring. Listen closely to what the person has to say and come back with relevant follow-up questions.

Work at being a good storyteller. Don't get stuck at the unnecessary details and pester someone with a boring story for half an hour. Make sure that what you're talking about will be interesting by telling the most important pieces in an entertaining way so that the person you're talking to becomes engaged.

If you notice that he or she gets bored, change topics and ask a question instead. When you talk about yourself, do it with a twinkle in the eye, dare to make fun of yourself without demeaning yourself. By daring to talk about both good things and small misadventures in your life, you show that you're confident in yourself and don't need any confirmation. It radiates self-assurance and self-confidence.

As you can see, it can sometimes be a bit tricky to communicate with others. For some, it's quite natural, for others it's a little more difficult. Even if you find it hard to connect with new people dare to overcome your fears. All acquaintances has once started as strangers and just by daring you have the opportunity to take part of all the interesting people that the world has to offer. One of the most fascinating individuals is yourself and your surroundings deserve to take note of you and what you have to say. And you know what, if another person isn't interested in talking to you, don't take it personal because they don't know you. Never forget that when someone doesn't want to let new people in their life, it's often because they're afraid. Don't let negative and anxious people affect your life. Stand tall and smile, for you are a person with a plan, you are one of the few in this world who actually dare to strive to fulfill your dreams. You are already on your way, you have dared to write down your goals in life, you have dared to make a plan to achieve them, and you dare to take small steps towards your goals every day.

Now is the time to wrap up your social goals. Go for it!

TASK: SOCIAL GOALS

Now is your chance to increase your social skills. Decide on one to three social goals that you will work towards in the immediate future. Don't forget to use the exercise earlier in the chapter where you wrote down some key words on how you want to be perceived by other people.

Before you set up your new social goals, answer these questions which can help you with your new goals:

» Are you afraid of rejection? If yes, what is it that makes you afraid of rejection?
» What do you want to improve with your body language?
» How can you get better at conveying what you want to say?
» How can you become a better listener?

These are tricky questions so take your time to respond. Hopefully, you have already found some social skills that you wish to improve. You can transform them into your new social goals. If you have any other social goals, it's perfectly okay. Remember that when it comes to your goals, it's always you who decide, but also you who will implement them. Follow these steps (which you probably recognize by now) to set your social goals.

» Write down at least one and maximum three social goals.
» Write down in a few lines what it will mean for your life when you achieve your goals.
» Set a deadline.
» Make an activity plan.
» Set sub-goals.
» Do something today that will take you towards your goal.

EXAMPLE

Goal: Get rid of my fear of approaching people.

By daring to make contact with new people, my life will improve in many ways. I will meet new interesting people and increase my chances of meeting someone who shares my values and interests. Life will be more fun and I will get more friends and contacts.

Deadline: Three months.

Activity plan:
- » Take a course in communication.
- » Read books on dating.
- » Approach new people every day.
- » Participate in at least one speed dating session.

Sub-goal 1: Within a month I have gotten a date.
Reward: A nice date.

Sub-goal 2: Within two months, I have attended at least one speed dating session.
Reward: Talk to at least twenty new people.

Ultimate Goal: Within three months, I have lost my fear of approaching new people.
Reward: First and foremost, the pleasure of daring to make contact and engage in conversation with the one I want. In addition to that, I will reward myself with a two-hour Thai massage.

To do today: Register for a communication course.

�✭✭

THE FUTURE

"The future belongs to those who believe in the beauty of their dreams."

/ Eleanor Roosevelt

It's said that when one door closes another one opens. Soon you've read the last page of this book and our journey together ends. But when the book is closed, many, many other doors will open for you, of that I'm convinced. For those of you who really have given this book a chance and dared to do all the exercises and tasks, a good life filled with new opportunities is waiting. My goal is that you will dare to fight for the life you want to live, not what your surroundings want. Dare to go your own way and believe in yourself.

If, by writing this book, I can help even one person to a better life, I have succeeded. Obviously, I hope that everyone who reads it will get something out of it, and if you've come this far, I know that you are a disciplined person who dares to strive for what you want even though it can sometimes feel scary. See the book as a guide to achieving your goals, take it out now and then when you feel that you want to get back on the right track in terms of your goals.

Feel free to contact me and tell me what you have achieved with the help of your strong will and the tools that you have received. You can find my e-mail address at the beginning of the book. But before closing the covers, I have a few final things that I want to share with you. Take a deep breath, relax and enjoy the last pages.

THE 80/20 PRINCIPLE

Life is not always fair. The best we can do to succeed in life is to learn the rules and follow them. That life is not fair also means that ordinary people like you and me can succeed with great things if we learn the rules. A principle that has helped me and many other people to be more successful in business, in sports and in life in general is the 80/20 principle.

In the early 1900s, the Italian economist Vilfredo Pareto created a mathematical formula describing the unequal distribution of wealth in Italy. It turned out that 20 percent of the population owned 80 percent of all wealth. In the 1940s, the business and management consultant Joseph M. Juran further developed this theory that later got called the 80/20 principle (also known as the Pareto Principle or the 80/20 rule).

It turned out that the distribution 80/20 often applied, regardless of which area was investigated. 80 percent of the result came from 20 percent of the efforts. Do you understand? Let's describe it again.

The 80/20 principle thus means that 80 percent of the result in your life comes from 20 percent of your efforts. This means that only one-fifth (20 percent) of your actions in life accounts for almost all of your results (80 percent). The same is true in business, sports, friendships, problems and more.

Let's look at a few examples to make it easier to understand. If we look closely at a company, it turns out that in many cases 20 percent of the customers stand for 80 percent of the revenue. Similarly, 80 percent of all complaints the company receives comes from 20 percent of the customers. Let's take another example from the sporting world. If we were to look at Zlatan Ibrahimovic (the world famous soccer player), it would appear that about 80 percent of everything he achieves on the field is derived from 20 percent of his efforts. Similarly,

20 percent of the salespeople of a company accounts for 80 percent of the sales, well the list goes on and on.

Knowing the 80/20 principle will make it easier for you to succeed. According to me there are two important things you should consider in order to achieve greater success by using the 80/20 principle:

DO YOUR BEST WITH THE 20 PERCENT THAT COUNTS

It's a great feeling that 20 percent of the efforts accounts for 80 percent of the results. This means that there is a lot of time to relax, have fun and not worry about performance. Learn to identify what affects your result and give everything to the 20 percent that counts, because that's what will give you 80 percent of the results in life.

FIND THE 20 PERCENT THAT GIVES YOU PROBLEMS IN LIFE AND REMOVE IT

Imagine that 80 percent of your problems in life come from 20 percent of your surroundings or things that you do. Find the factors that influence things to not go as you wish and remove them from your life.

If you never heard of the 80/20 principle before it might sound strange and complicated but it's not. The only thing you need to consider is to do your best with the things that you feel gives results. The things that are not producing any results and cause problems you simply remove. Never forget the 80/20 principle, it will help you to get where you want in life.

PERSISTENT OR STUPID?

Do you know what the difference is between being persistent and being stupid? There can sometimes be a fine line between being persistent or stupid but the difference is still very significant. A stupid person who has decided on something continu-

&ce; ☆ &ce;

LIFE IS NOT
ALWAYS FAIR.
The best we can do
to succeed in life
is to learn the rules
and follow them.

es even if what he or she is doing is wrong. A persistent person however, gives everything and fights but have the knowledge to see if what he or she is doing is wrong and change it as required to make it right to continue forward. Sometimes it's easy to become blind and continue to do the same error day after day without thinking about it.

Imagine that you are a builder and will build a house for a customer. Everything starts off well and you add brick after brick until one morning you notice that what you built looks a bit crooked. When you look closer, you see that the ground is tilting and that you've built wrong. It doesn't take any *rocket science* to understand that in this situation it's time to start over and make it right. Similarly, you will also make mistakes in life sometimes. It's OK, everyone makes mistakes and it's through them we learn what doesn't work. The difference between those who succeed and those who fail is precisely the ability to recognize when you are wrong and adjust it as necessary to succeed.

Once you have found the recipe for success in the field you wish, you just have to do your homework every day, then you will succeed.

Remember that now you are a person who has a plan in your life. You have goals you are working towards every day. That is something to be proud of. Dare to change your goals and actions along the way if it's required for you to succeed. Just don't forget what the difference between being persistent and being stupid is. Sometimes you will notice along the way that the goal that you have set up no longer feels attractive. Be honest with yourself and have the courage to change it and aim for a new goal. But don't give up just because it's hard, continue forward, you'll make it.

WHEN ARE YOU SATISFIED?

How is it that some people seem to have everything but still don't seem happy and that others don't seem to have anything but still appears to be the happiest in the world?

My roots are from Macedonia, a very beautiful country in Southeastern Europe. Macedonia has a green and mountainous countryside and can boast with one of the world's oldest and deepest inland lakes. It's one of Europe's poorer countries, yet I have never seen more happiness than during the summers that I spent with my grandparents there. The people don't have much to boast about when it comes to the material things or financially, but they are very rich in terms of the family. The neighbors are often like family members, there is always time for a coffee or a little meze (appetizers/snacks). The doors are open and there are often parties. Weddings and holidays are celebrated and everyone is fighting for a better tomorrow. Although these people are struggling financially they seem very happy.

On the other hand, I'm born and raised in Sweden, a country often praised as one of the best countries in the world to live in. In Sweden we have free healthcare, free university and the list goes on, but often we take it for granted and it gives us no greater happiness. Now I live in America just because I want to spread my message and pursue my own dreams and goals of being successful here. Wherever you might live today you can be a winner; there are opportunities and a good future, but you must feel that it is like that. Your happiness depends on you and how you choose to look at things.

SO THE QUESTION IS, WHEN ARE YOU SATISFIED?

Some believe that a satisfied person can never reach what he or she really wants because they are already happy with life. I absolutely disagree. Just because you're happy doesn't mean that you don't want to continue fighting. I think that even if you're satisfied with what you have, you can always strive forward. By setting new goals, you keep the fire going within you.

Don't make it so hard for yourself to succeed in life. Be glad for the small things, but aim for the big ones. Don't be a person who has everything but is still not satisfied. Every day you wake up is a new day that will never come back. Bring out your smile and make something good out of that day. Life is meant to be lived. Do your best and have fun along the way, it will take you far in life. And hey, don't take life too seriously. Make something good out of the short time you have here on earth.

DON'T FORGET THE JOURNEY

One of America's best gymnasts was once asked what would happen if he never was selected for the Olympics and never won the gold. How do you think he reacted? He got angry and began to yell: "What do you mean if I fail?"

Do you dare to live with the thought of what happens if you would fail? For me life is about developing yourself to such a level that you dare to have big dreams and really give everything and fight for them. But we must be sure to have fun along the way towards the goals and accept that we may not always be successful in achieving exactly what we want.

When I look back on everything I have achieved in my life it's not the success itself that pleases me, but the journey to get there. All the people I've met, all the places I've been to and all the things I have learned. Don't make the mistake that many people make when they pursue a dream all their life and forget to have fun in the meantime. They forsake their surroundings and themselves. Some succeed, others don't, but regardless of which it's the way there that is the most fun, I can vouch for that. I have managed to accomplish to win a World Championship medal in Shotokan karate. A dream came true after twenty years of training. The first few days I felt like a king, I was floating on a cloud and I was extremely happy. We were in Sydney, Australia, the sun was shining and after having trained all my life, I managed to perform when it really mattered. It's a wonderful feeling when everything goes your way and it lifts you to a level you never thought existed. But after a few days we traveled home and eventually everyday life came back. In a way, everything had changed, but at the same time nothing really changed. I still need to work and life goes on. I'm still the same person as before, but now with a piece of metal on a string in a glass cabinet in my living room. A few weeks after the competition I was fired from my job when the product I worked for was dropped. At that time it was like no one cared that I was a bronze medalist in a World Championship. Fortunately, I fought for myself and not for others' acknowledgment. I've learned to enjoy the journey and have fun along the way.

For many, there is an emptiness after they have fought very long for something. Don't make that mistake, have fun and don't take everything so serious. Make friends, laugh and cry. Lick your wounds and move on. Turn a problem into an opportunity. Life is a journey, not a destination, every day counts, make it count!

DO YOUR HOMEWORK

I hope you by now have received many tools that will help you create the life you desire in the future. Some of the ideas I have given you will stick more than others, but if I had to choose just one thing that you should take with you from this book it's the importance of doing your homework. No matter what you want to achieve and how you want to live your life it is within reach as long as you do your homework. Many things in life can seem very difficult to achieve until they are divided into small, small daily steps. Suddenly that "unattainable thing" is within reach.

Whether you want to become a millionaire, lawyer, lose 50 pounds or build a hut with your bare hands, everything is actually possible to achieve. If anyone else has done it before, you have proof that it's possible, and if no one hasn't yet succeeded, they haven't found the right path. You can find it, every day people accomplish something that nobody else has ever done before. Everything is achievable for anyone who is willing to have the discipline to take small steps every day towards their goals.

Many people try to take a shortcut to success and happiness. The harsh truth is that to succeed, no matter in which field it may be, it requires work. It's required that you are willing to spend time on what you want to achieve. Quick fixes and shortcuts can help you a bit, but they can never take you all the way. A fact that leads many people to give up – but not you! If you have come this far, I know that you can succeed. You have the discipline and desire. And the best part of the fact that daily work is needed for a long time in order to succeed is that anyone can succeed at almost anything as long as they have the discipline and desire.

Have you heard the story of the tortoise and the hare? A story about that you should always do your best. Many times things can turn out well in life, even if you don't believe it.

Once upon a time, there was a tortoise and a hare. The hare was jumping around and playing in the leaves and bushes. He ran here and there and tasted as many different plants that he could find. The tortoise was calmly looking for the leaves that he recognized and ate them.

"How slow you're crawling," said the hare to the tortoise.

"Oh, you think so," said the tortoise.

"Yes, you won't get anywhere as slow as you are."

"Yes, but I'm getting where I want to go," said the tortoise.

"Oh, but you can never participate in any contest. You would always come last," said the hare and laughed and waved his long ears.

"If you want we can organize a race and compete against each other. The one who comes first wins," said the tortoise.

"I'm on," said the hare.

The tortoise and the hare appointed a jury of a lion, an elephant and a giraffe. They decided the start and finish line for the race and that the competition would take place the next day in a place that was right by the river. The hare thought it would be fun to win the race. Everyone would cheer for him.

Tomorrow came, and it was time for the race. A large audience of various animals gathered to watch.

The tortoise and the hare lined up next to each other at the starting line. The hare shook his long ears.

"This will be an easy race," he thought, looking down at the tortoise. "It's enough if I start a bit later. I can sleep at the beginning of the competition. I just need to take a few leaps with my long legs and I will reach the goal."

The tortoise looked very determined under his hard shell. The starting signal went off and the race started.

The hare took a few leaps and laid down to rest behind a bush.

The tortoise began to crawl as fast as he could. He didn't stop to rest for a single second. He crawled and crawled – up on the rocks and down into the pits. Sometimes he stumbled and nearly tipped over on his back. But he turned himself right again and went on and on towards the goal. It didn't go fast, but the goal slowly came closer.

The animals that stood and watched got very surprised. They didn't believe that a tortoise could crawl so far. The hare was nowhere to be seen. All the animals thought it was ama-

ᘒ ☆ ᘒ

YOU SHOULD ALWAYS DO YOUR BEST.

*It may go well
even if you don't believe it.
Anyone who tries can win.*

zing that the tortoise had come so far. Now he had passed the midline. "Go tortoise" they shouted. "Go, go! The tortoise might win."

They applauded and shouted so loudly that the hare woke up. He had fallen asleep behind the bush. But now he woke up with full steam. He jumped up and skipped away towards the goal.

But the tortoise kept gaining speed. Every time he heard how the animals screamed and cheered him he crawled a little faster.

The hare hopped and skipped. Now he was almost at the river's edge and the goal.

But just at that second the tortoise crawled across the finish line. "The tortoise has reached the goal! The tortoise is the winner! Hurrah, hurrah!" shouted all the animals.

The lion, who was the leader of the jury, shouted loudly so that everyone could hear: "The tortoise has won the race. The hare has lost."

The giraffe and the elephant lifted up the tortoise. They let him drink from the river and then they carried him so that everyone could see the winner. All the animals cheered and congratulated.

Everyone was happy except the hare. He had been so confident of winning that he had not bothered to make any effort. But then things can go bad. You should always do your best. It may go well even if you don't believe it. Anyone who tries can win.

The story of the tortoise and the hare is a perfect example that anyone can succeed. The key is to do your homework. By daring to try and do your best, you can go far.

HELP OTHERS

"If you wanna make the world a better place, take a look at yourself, and then make a change."

These words are some of the strongest that have ever been sung in a song. "Man in the Mirror", as you probably have heard many times, is written by the legendary Michael Jackson. If you want to make the world a better place, you have to start with yourself. Remember that you are a successful person with dreams and goals, you are a role model for other people. Be proud of yourself. But with success comes a responsibility. Just as you have been helped by me and many other people, it's time for you to give a helping hand. There are many ways to help other people to enjoy a better life. You can help with your knowledge, your time, your money or your commitment.

Dare to help other people, you will notice that there is nothing more rewarding than getting your fellow human beings to feel better. Many live with the belief that in order for them to have a good life, someone else must have a bad one. That's not true, there are resources for everyone on this planet. Unfortunately they are a little skewed, but you and I can do our part to make this planet a better place.

Get involved so other people can get it better. You can teach them about goals in life or share any other knowledge that you have. You can donate your old clothes so someone else doesn't have to freeze. You can avoid throwing away food out of respect for those who are hungry. You can donate money to charity, or why not go and help someone yourself. It's just your imagination that sets the limits.

The important thing is that you learn to be a generous person. Don't think that success in life is limited, on the contrary, everyone can succeed if we only help each other. Everyone can be winners in life. Never forget that the one who gives is also the one who receives. Everyone deserves to have a good life, be sure to do your part. Dare to create the life you deserve and have the courage to help others to reach were they want to go.

LAST BUT NOT LEAST

You are welcome! That was all I had to say for now. I want to thank you for this time we have had together. I hope that one day we can meet so I can take part of your journey towards the life you desire. Dare to go your own way, dare to believe in yourself! I know you can succeed. You know the recipe at this point, but let me remind you one last time: Write down your goals, set a deadline, make an activity plan, set sub-goals and do something today that will take you closer to what you want. Then you just have to do your daily homework. It's actually no harder than that.

Best wishes from the bottom of my heart.

AFTERWORD

The summer is approaching here on the west coast of Sweden. The sun is shining, the birds are singing and today the wind blows like it can only blow here on the west coast. I'm sitting right where I started a little over a month ago, in perhaps the most beautiful library we have in Sweden. I sit alone by the same gray table and the four green chairs where I started.

The view is still the beautiful river Nissan, but today the sky is bluer than it was when I started.

Who knew that I would, in just over 30 days, write a book about living a life of happiness, well-being and wealth? Although I hardly believed myself that I could succeed in this short time, I know exactly why I did. The goal was to write at least two pages every day and that is exactly what I have done. Some days it was easy to write two pages of text, other days I had to work hard for many hours. During this month I have become part of the inventory at this city library. There have been many cups of cappuccino with a double shot of espresso from the library café. There have been many sleepless nights as I have been thinking about how I best can convey my message.

I'm proud of what I've accomplished. By doing my homework every day, I have created a book that can help you live the life you desire.

Before taking leave of my friends, the gray table and its four green chairs for the last time, I'll just have to share with you what I now have realized: If a regular guy like me can succeed, I know that you also can succeed!

/Peter Jumrukovski